ALFRED'S BASIC GUITAR ROCK SONGS METHOD 1

OVER FIVE MILLION COPIES SOLD

AB

LEARN HOW TO PLAY GUITAR WITH MELODIES AND RIFFS FROM 22 CLASSIC ROCK SONGS

For individual or class instruction

NATHANIEL GUNOD
L. C. HARNSBERGER
RON MANUS

Satisfy your desire to learn rock guitar with this unique method that gets you started by teaching some of the greatest rock songs of all time. Playing melodies and riffs from these great songs will reinforce techniques and inspire you to continue learning. So don't wait–start rockin' now!

In addition to video lessons, the companion DVD includes Alfred's exclusive TNT 2 software, which allows users to customize the audio tracks in this book for practice. Use it to slow down tracks, isolate and loop parts, and change tempos and keys. To install, insert the DVD into the disc drive of your computer.

PC
Double-click on **My Computer**, right-click on the DVD drive icon, and select **Explore**. Open the **DVD-ROM Materials** folder, then the **TNT2** folder, then the PC folder, and double-click on the installer file.

Mac
Double-click on the DVD icon on your desktop. Open the **DVD-ROM Materials** folder, then the **TNT2** folder, then the **Mac** folder, and double-click on the installer file.

TNT2 SYSTEM REQUIREMENTS

Windows
7, 8, 10
QuickTime 7.6.7 or higher
1.8 GHz processor or faster
900 MB hard drive space
2 GB RAM minimum
DVD drive for installation
Speakers or headphones
Internet access for updates

Macintosh
OS 10.4 and higher (Intel only)
QuickTime 7.6.7or higher
900 MB hard drive space
2 GB RAM minimum
DVD drive for installation
Speakers or headphones
Internet access for updates

Alfred Music
P.O. Box 10003
Van Nuys, CA 91410-0003
alfred.com

Book & DVD & Online Video/Audio/Software
ISBN-10: 1-4706-3766-9
ISBN-13: 978-1-4706-3766-8

Front cover photos:
Gibson SGSR-VOFCNH1 courtesy of Gibson USA • Guitar player photo © GettyImages_Dutko

Back cover photo models:
Janet Robin (top), janetrobin.com • Paris Carney (middle left), pariscarney.com • Luis Cabezas from The Dollyrots (middle right), thedollyrots.com

Back cover photos:
Top three photos: Kevin Estrada • Bottom photo: © Wolfgang Lienbacher / Vetta / Getty Images

Alfred Cares. Contents printed on environmentally responsible paper.

Contents

The Parts of Your Guitar

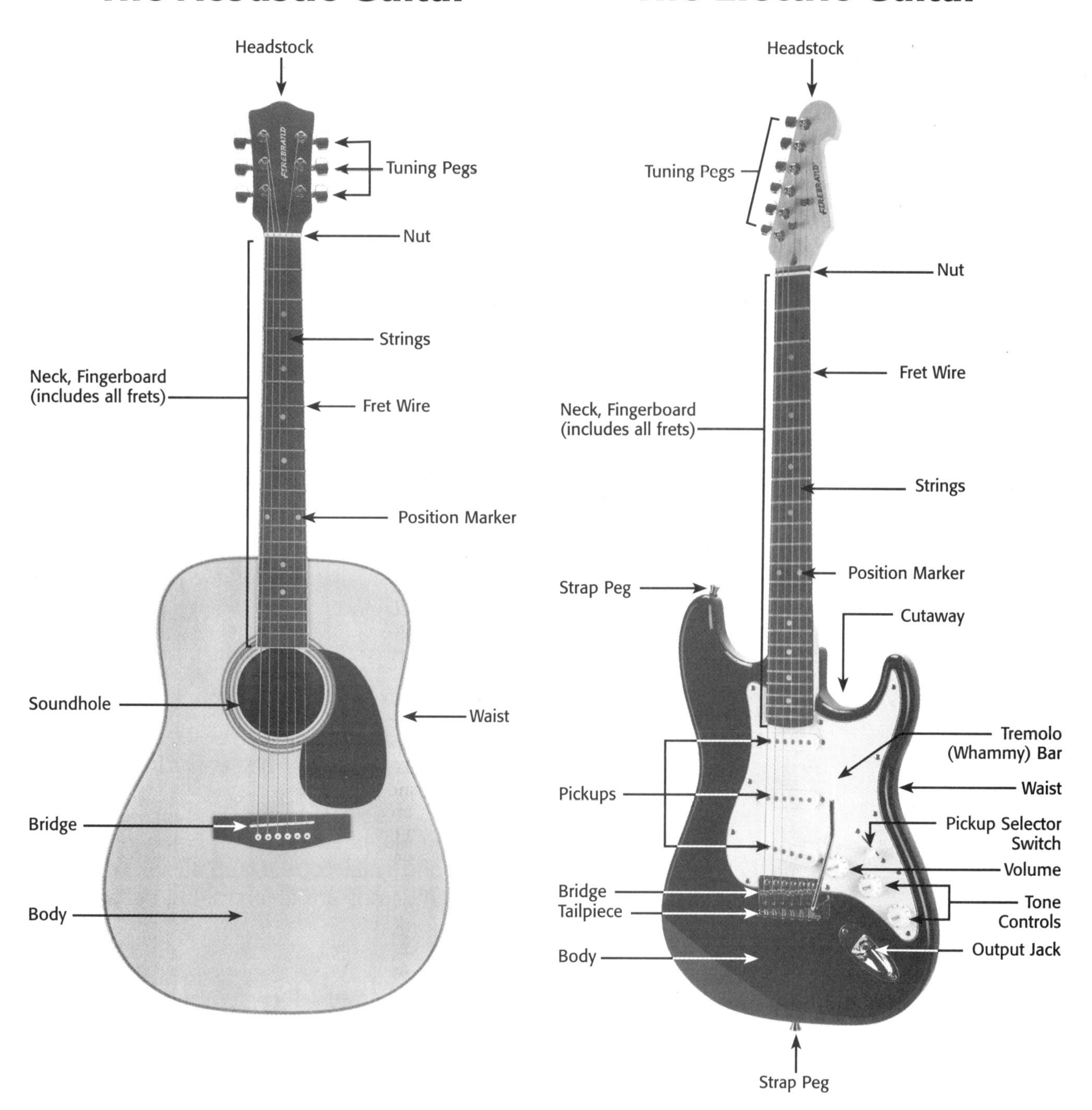

Which Guitar Is Best for Me?

Should you use an acoustic or electric guitar? It's all a matter of taste. Choose a guitar based on what kind of music you want to play and what you want to sound like. The most important consideration is probably the size: if you have small hands, you will find a smaller guitar easier to play. Also, a guitar with a very big, fat body will be hard for a small person to hold. If you want to rock out, start learning on an electric guitar—there are no rules about which guitar to get first. Get one that you will want to pick up and play every day!

How to Hold Your Guitar

Hold your guitar in a position that is most comfortable for you. Some positions are shown below.

When playing, keep your left wrist away from the fingerboard. This will allow your fingers to be in a better position to play the strings. Press your fingers firmly, but make sure they do not touch the neighboring strings.

Tilt the neck slightly up. Don't twist the body of the guitar to see the strings better.

Standing with strap.

Sitting.

Sitting with legs crossed.

The Amplifier

If you are playing an electric guitar, you will need to use an *amplifier*. The amplifier (or amp) makes the sound of a guitar louder, and allows you to add effects, like distortion, to your sound. All amps are different, but here are a few features you will find on most amps.

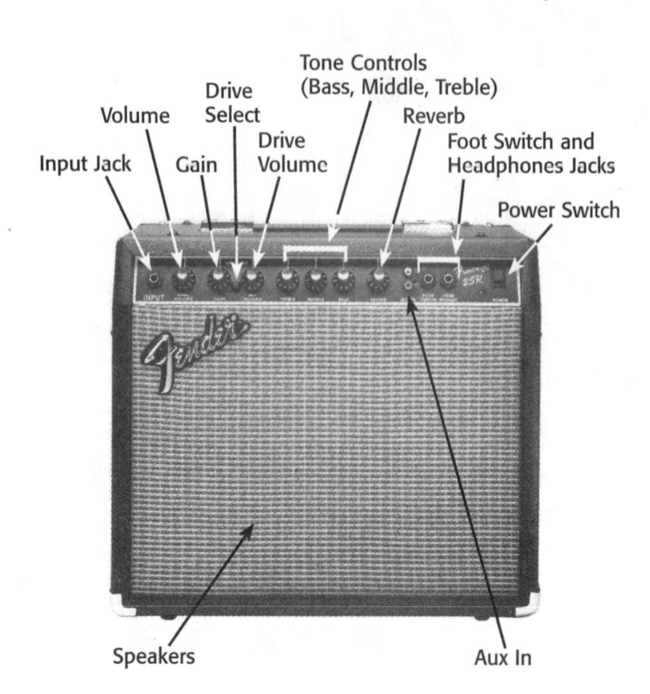

Aux In: RCA input jacks for use with an auxiliary audio source.

Input Jacks: Where you plug in your guitar.

Drive Select: Activates the Drive channel.

Drive Volume: Controls the loudness of the Drive channel.

Foot Switch and Headphones Jacks: For plugging in an optional foot switch for changing channels, or headphones for practicing.

Gain: Sometimes called "drive," will adjust the amount distortion added to your sound.

Power Switch: Turns the unit on and off.

Reverb: Adds an echo sound to your playing, not all amps have this feature.

Speakers: Where sound comes out of the amp.

Tone Controls: Used to adjust the bass (low), middle, and treble (high) sounds of your guitar.

Volume: Used to adjust the loudness of your amp; the higher the number, the louder the sound.

How to Tune Your Guitar

First, make sure your strings are wound properly around the tuning pegs. They should go from the inside to the outside as illustrated to the right. Some guitars have all six tuning pegs on the same side of the headstock. If this is the case, make sure all six strings are wound the same way, from the inside out.

Turning a tuning peg clockwise makes the string looser and the pitch lower. Turning a tuning peg counterclockwise makes the string tighter and the pitch higher. Be sure not to tighten the strings too much because they could break. Always pluck the string and listen as you turn the tuning pegs.

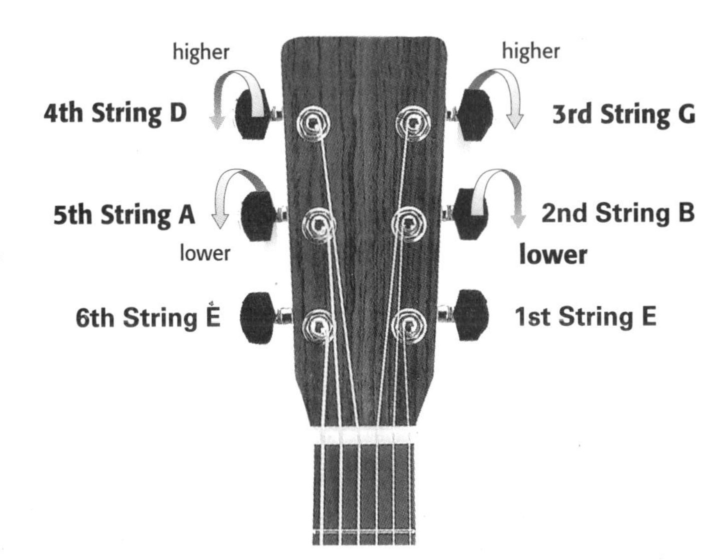

Important

Always remember that the thinnest, highest-sounding string, the one closest to the floor, is the 1st string. The thickest, lowest-sounding string, the one closest to the ceiling, is the 6th string. When guitarists say "the highest string," they are referring to the highest-sounding string.

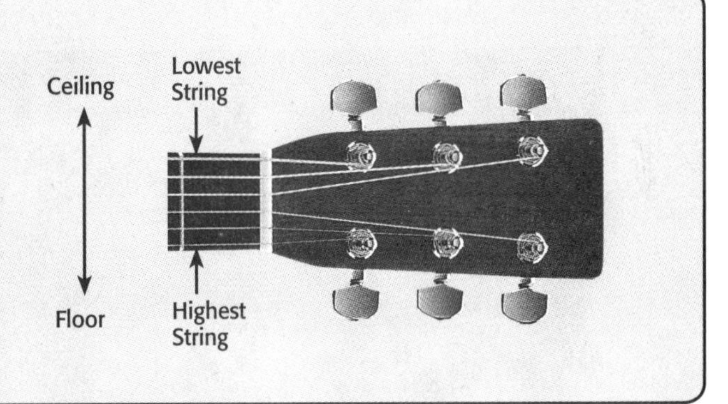

Tuning the Guitar to Itself

Tune the 6th string to E on the keyboard. If no keyboard is available, approximate E as best as you can and proceed as follows:

Press 5th fret of 6th string to get pitch of 5th string (A).

Press 5th fret of 5th string to get pitch of 4th string (D).

Press 5th fret of 4th string to get pitch of 3rd string (G).

Press 4th fret of 3rd string to get pitch of 2nd string (B).

Press 5th fret of 2nd string to get pitch of 1st string (E).

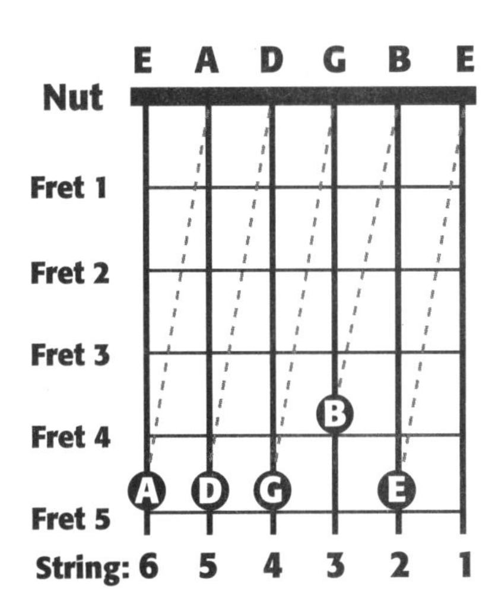

How to Use an Electronic Tuner

An electronic tuner is a handy device that can help keep your guitar in tune. You pick each string one at a time, and the tuner will guide you to the exact pitch the string should be for it to be in tune. Until your ear is more experienced, an electronic tuner can be extremely useful.

Tuning with the Audio or Video

Track 1

To tune while listening to the audio tracks or watching the video, follow the directions and match each of your strings to the corresponding pitches.

The Right Hand

Strumming with a Pick

Hold the pick between your thumb and index finger. Grip it firmly, but don't squeeze too hard.

Strum from the 6th string (the thickest, lowest-sounding string) to the 1st string (the thinnest, highest-sounding string).

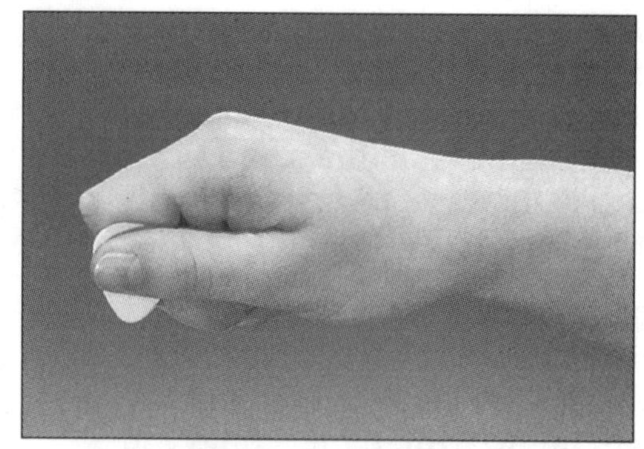

Correct way to hold a pick.

Important: Strum by mostly moving your wrist, not just your arm. Use as little motion as possible. Start as close to the 6th string as you can, and never let your hand move past the edge of the guitar.

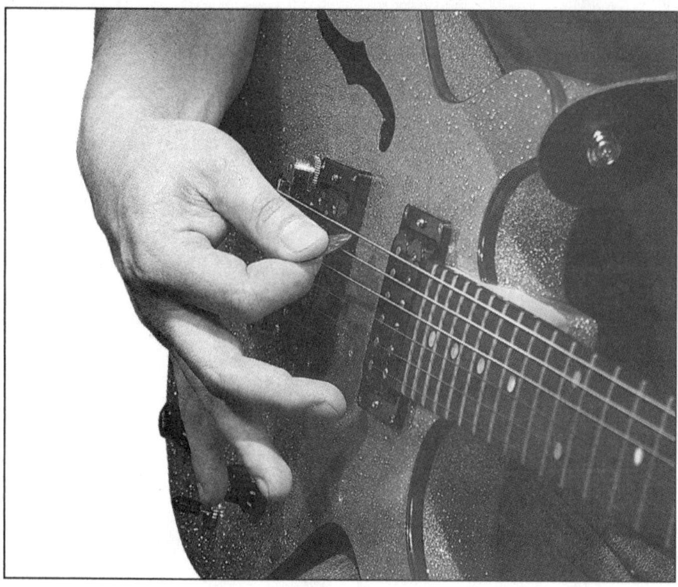

Start near the 6th string.

Move mostly your wrist, not just your arm.
Finish near the 1st string.

The Left Hand

Proper Left-Hand Position

Learning to use your left-hand fingers starts with good hand position. Place your hand so your thumb rests comfortably in the middle of the back of the neck. Position your fingers on the strings as if you are gently squeezing a ball between your fingers and thumb. Keep your elbow in and your fingers curved.

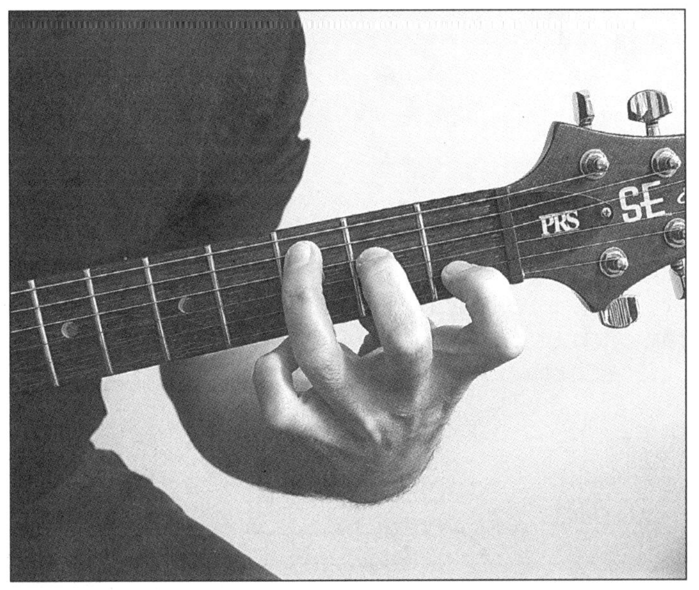

With your elbow in and fingers curved, arch your wrist slightly so your fingertips can more easily come down on top of the strings.

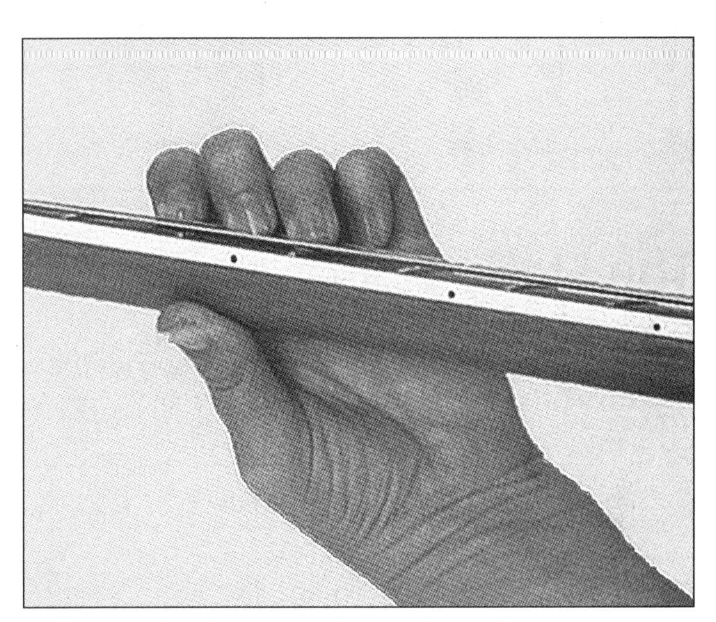

Position yourself as if you are gently squeezing a ball between your fingertips and thumb. Place the thumb behind the fingerboard opposite the middle finger.

Placing a Finger on a String

When you press a string with a left-hand finger, make sure to press firmly with the tip of your finger as close to the fret wire as you can without actually being right on it. This will create a clean, bright tone.

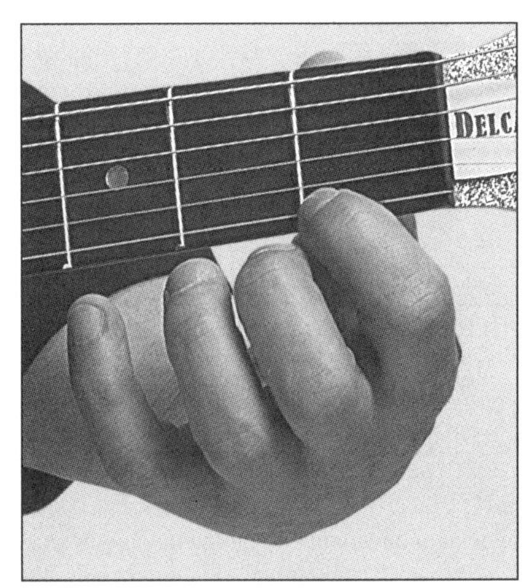

Right!
Finger presses the string down near the fret without actually being on it.

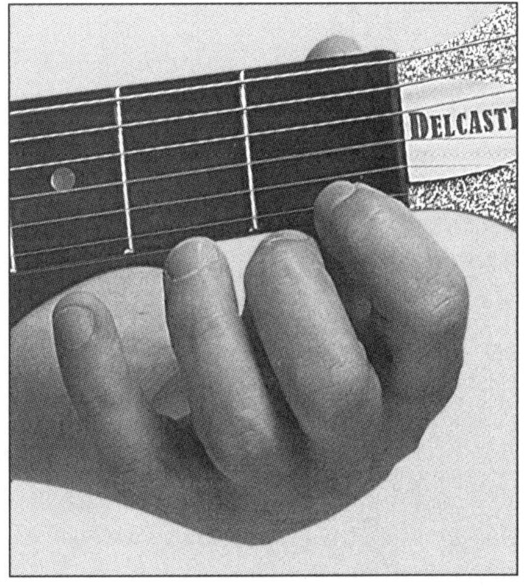

Wrong!
Finger is too far from the fret wire; the tone is "buzzy" and indefinite.

Wrong!
Finger is on top of the fret wire; the tone is muffled and unclear.

Getting Acquainted with Music

Musical sounds are indicated by symbols called *notes*. Their time value is determined by their color (white or black) and by *stems* or *flags* attached to the *note head*.

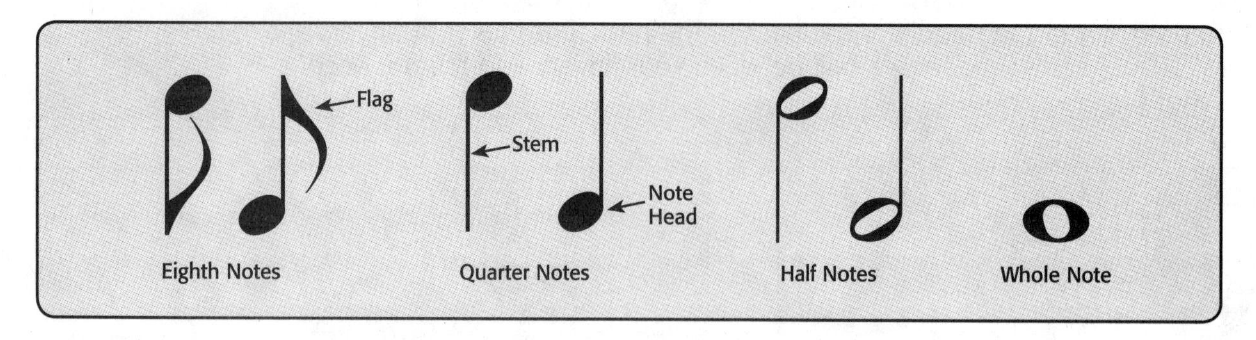

The Staff

Notes are named after the first seven letters of the alphabet (A–G), endlessly repeated to embrace the entire range of musical sound. The name and pitch of the note is determined by its position on five horizontal lines and the spaces between, called the *staff*.

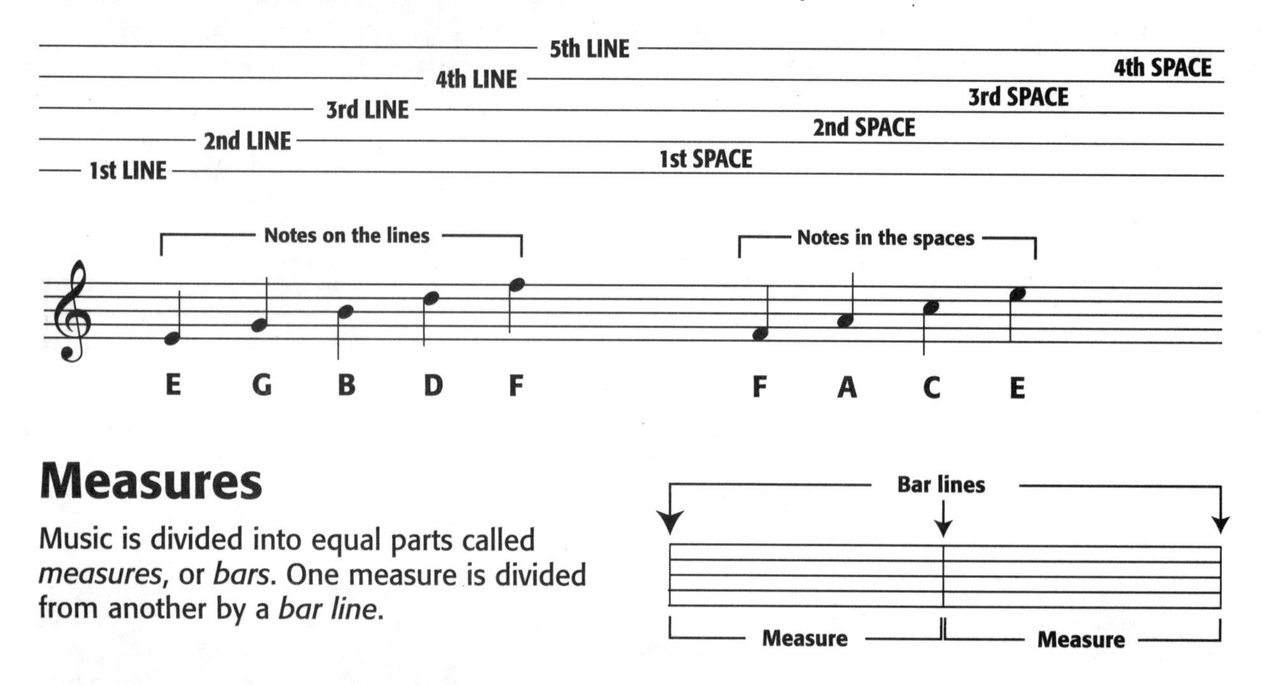

Measures

Music is divided into equal parts called *measures*, or *bars*. One measure is divided from another by a *bar line*.

Clefs

During the evolution of musical notation, the staff had from 2 to 20 lines, and symbols were invented to locate certain lines and the pitch of the note on that line. These symbols are called *clefs*. Music for guitar is written in the *G clef*, or *treble clef*.

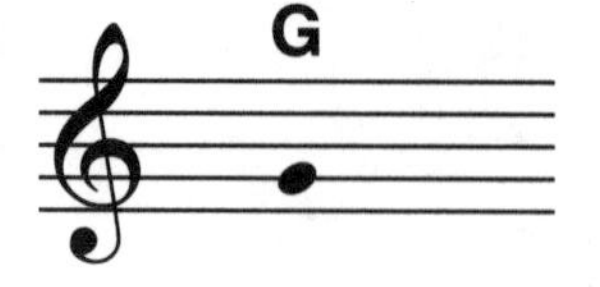

How to Read Chord Diagrams

Chord diagrams show where to place your left-hand fingers. Strings not played are shown with dashed lines and an X. The number within the circle indicates the left-hand finger that is pressed down.

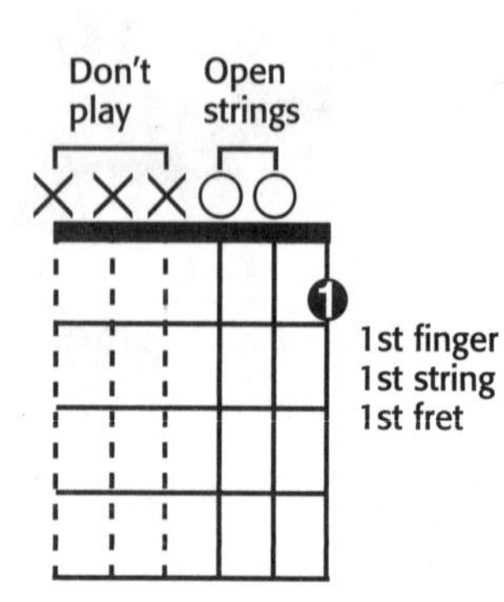

The 6th String E

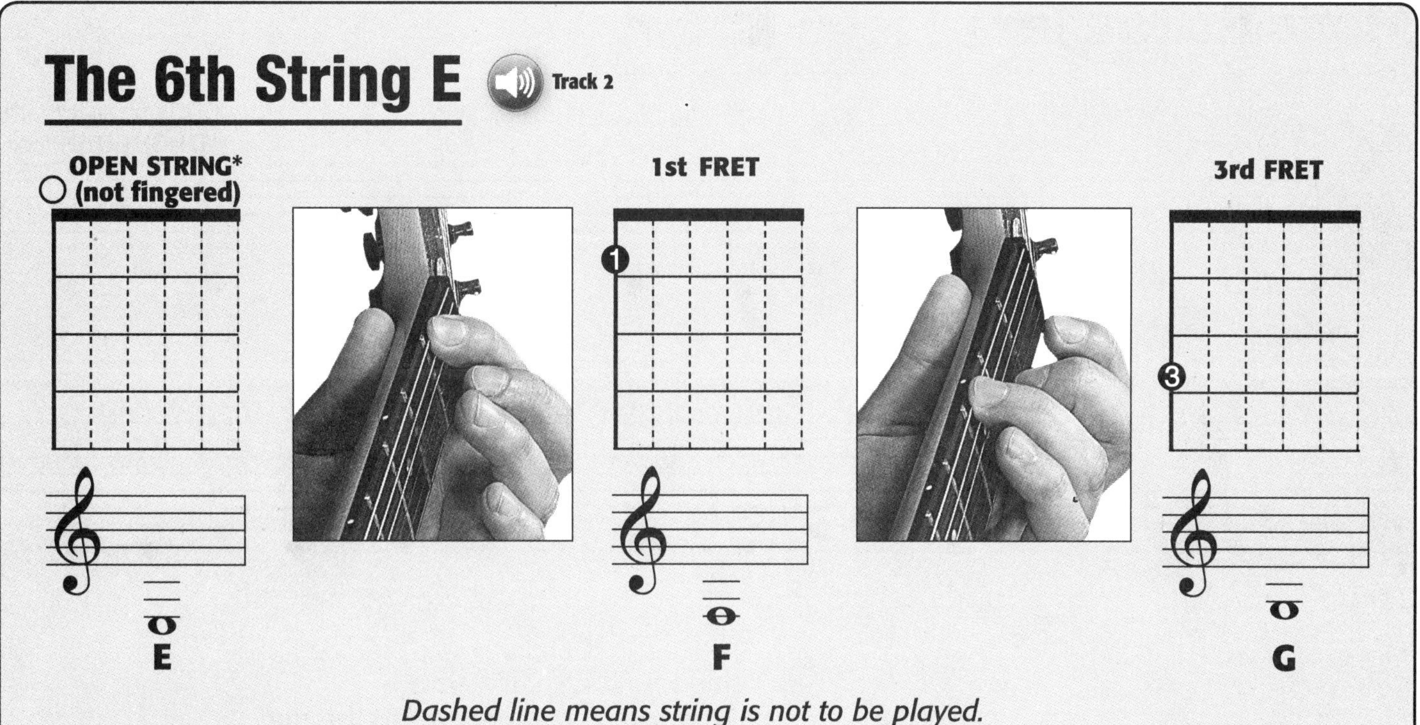

Dashed line means string is not to be played.

It is easy to tell the notes E, F, and G apart. E is the note under the three lines below the staff. F is on the third line below the staff. G is under the two lines below the staff.

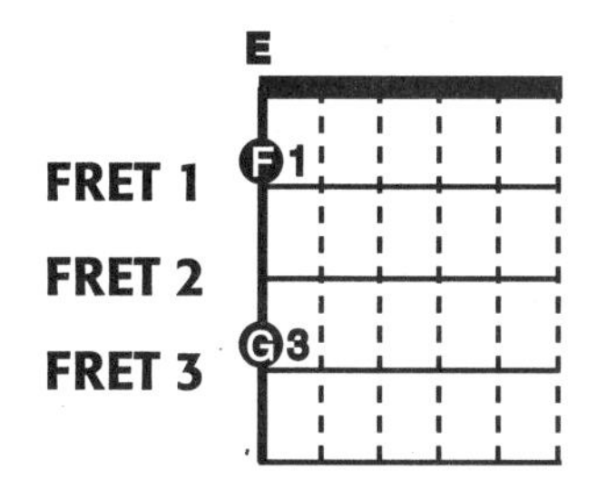

Use only *down-strokes*, indicated by ⊓, which means to pick down towards the floor. The symbol ○ under or over a note means *open string.* Do not finger.

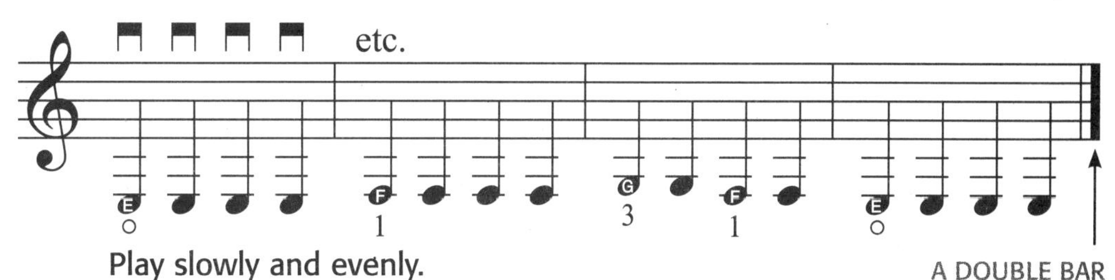

Play slowly and evenly.

A DOUBLE BAR INDICATES THE END OF AN EXAMPLE OR SONG.

6th-String Riff 1

A *riff* is a short, repeated melodic pattern.

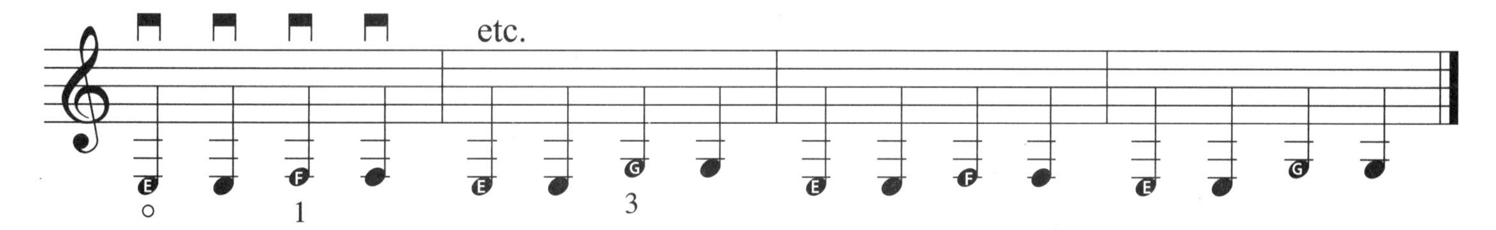

6th-String Riff 2

Track 4

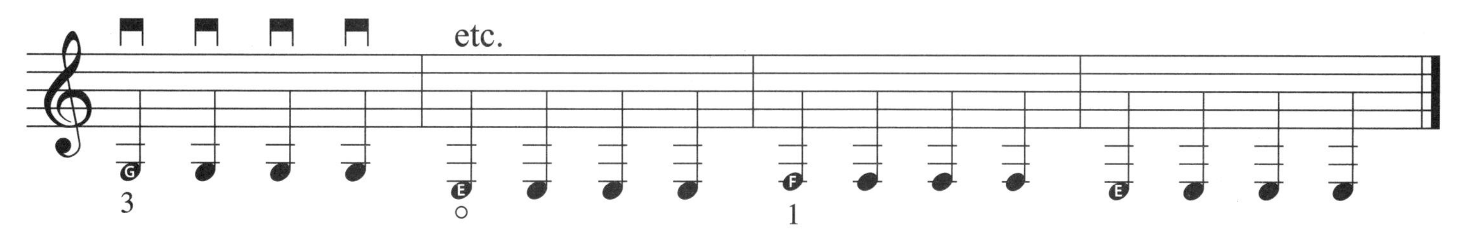

* Though there is no photo for the open string, the left-hand fingers should remain slightly above the string, ready to play the next fretted note. The thumb should always remain in its proper position.

More Riffs

Track 5

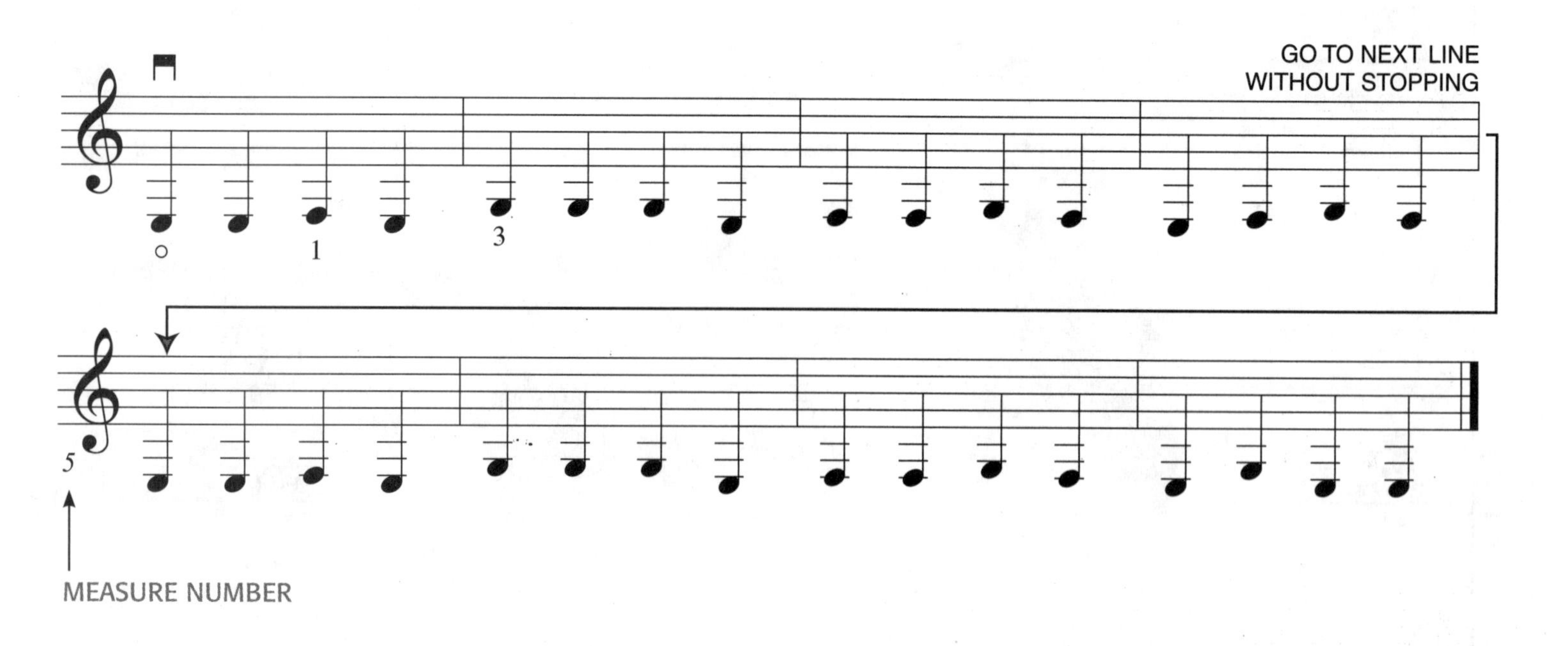

Still More Riffs

Track 6

Rockin' Bass Line Track 7

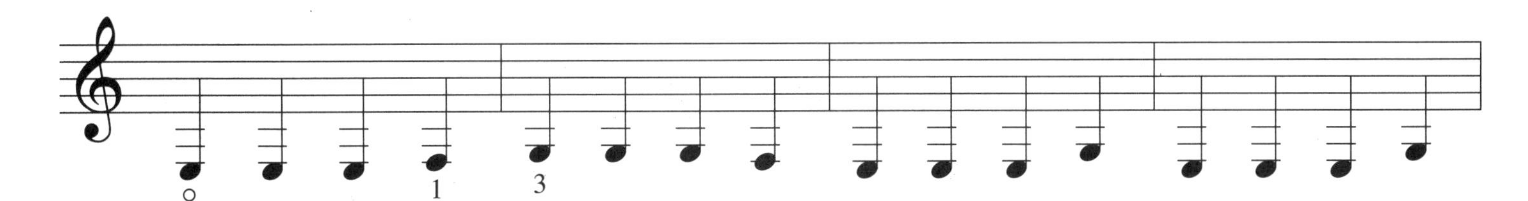

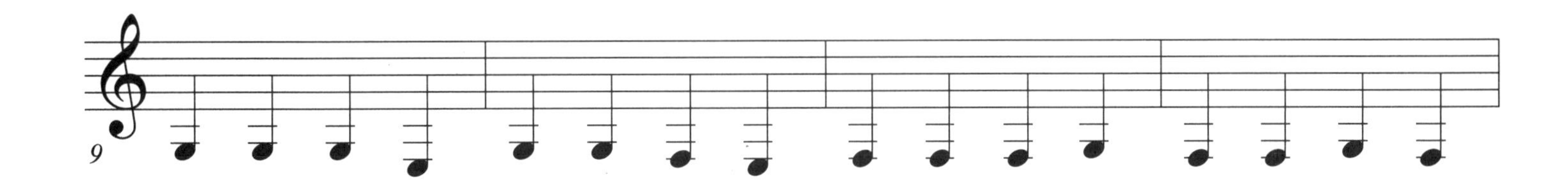

Silent Guitar Calisthenics 1 and 2

This exercise is silent because it is done with only the left hand. The goal is to go as slowly as possible with one finger down on the string as you add the other. Press the string down more firmly than usual. You are working the muscles that spread the fingers apart, and this will help develop that. Use the left side of the tip of your 1st finger and the middle of the tip of your 3rd finger. Remember to place the fingers just behind the frets.

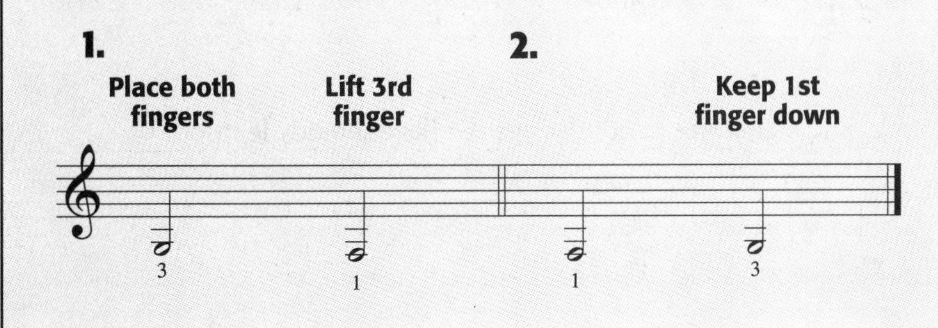

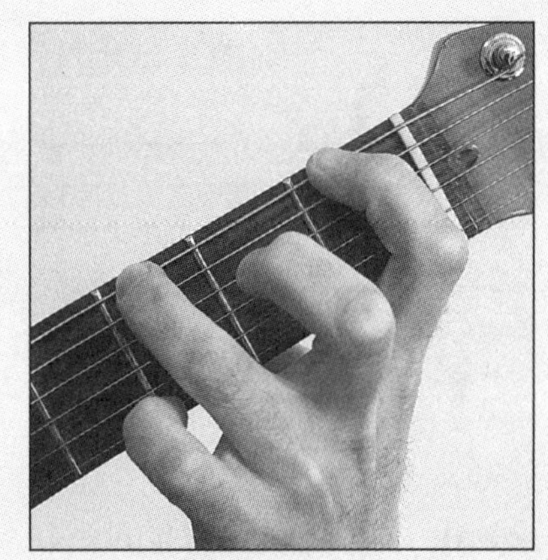

When both fingers are down, they should look similar to this.

Sound-Off: How to Count Time

Four Kinds of Notes

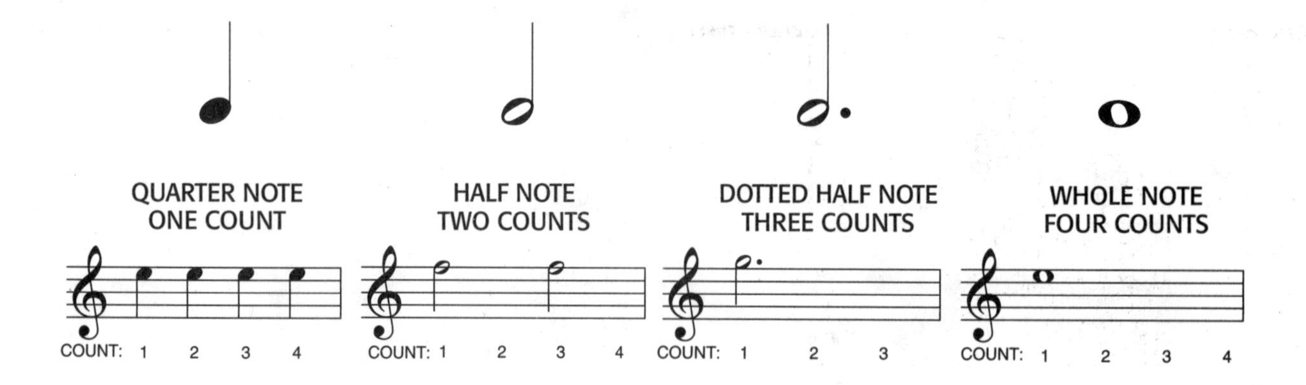

Time Signatures

Each piece of music has numbers at the beginning called a *time signature*. These numbers tell us how to count time.

The TOP NUMBER tells us how many counts are in each measure.
The BOTTOM NUMBER tells us what kind of note gets one count.

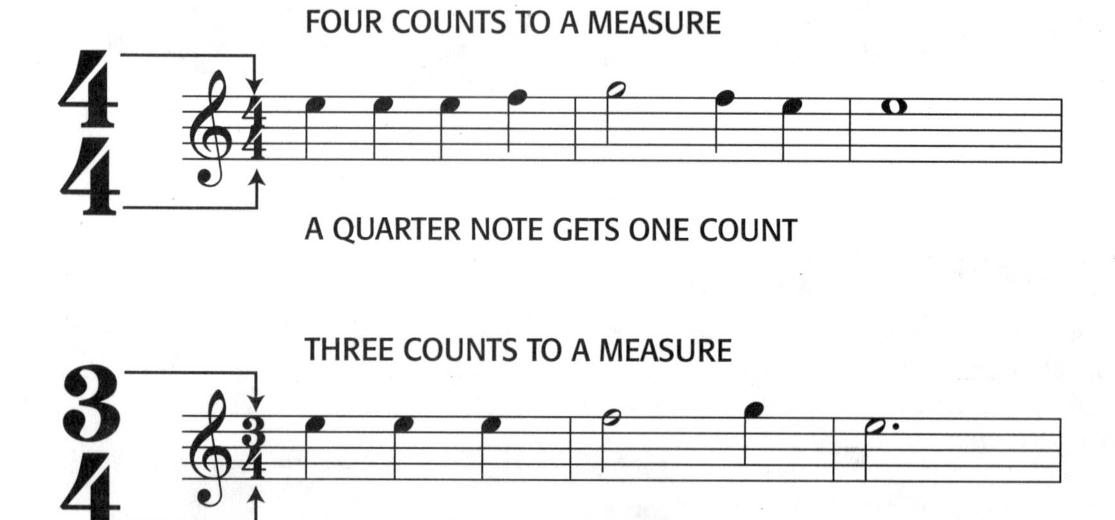

Important: Go back and fill in the missing time signatures for the songs we have already learned.

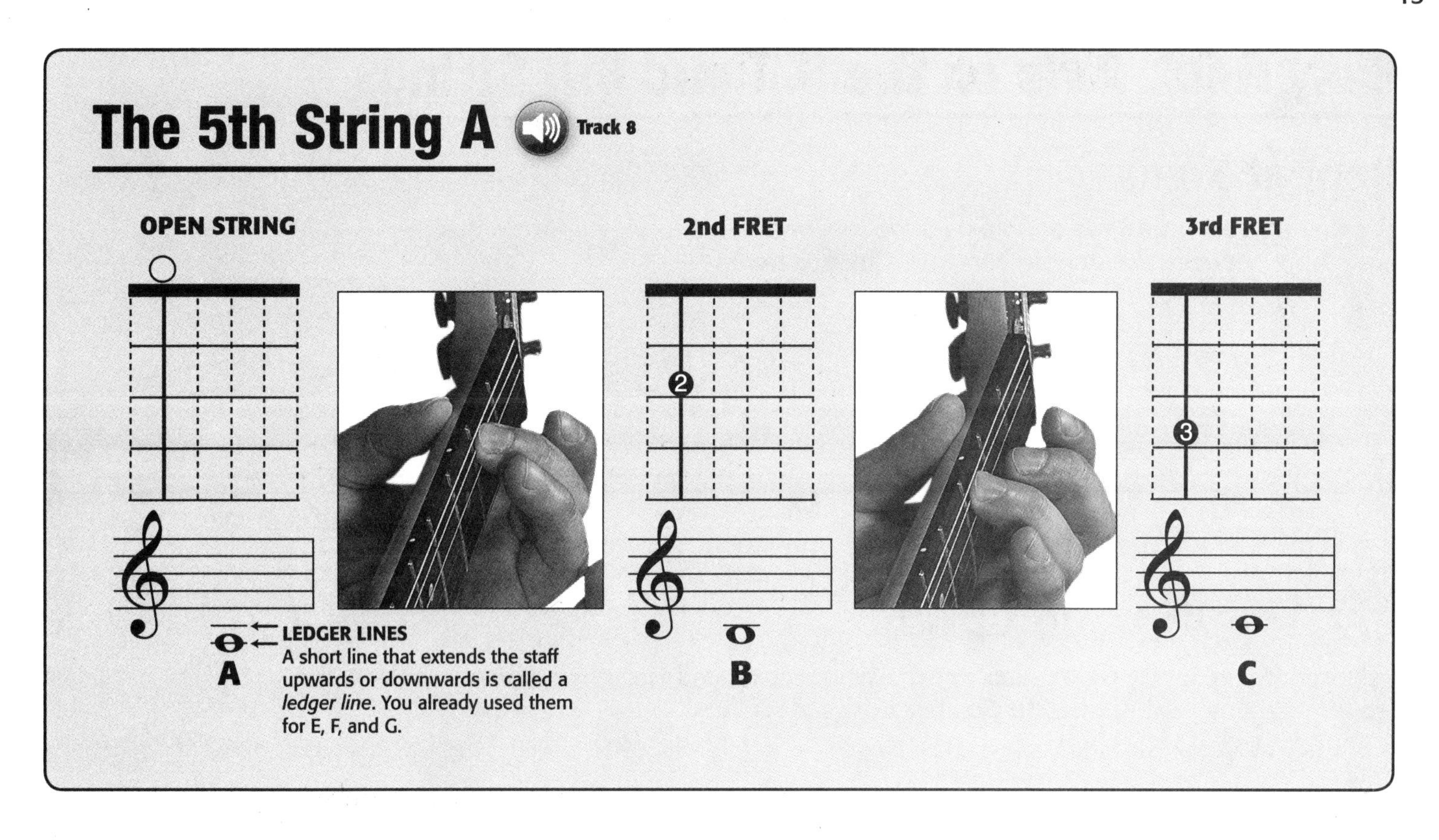

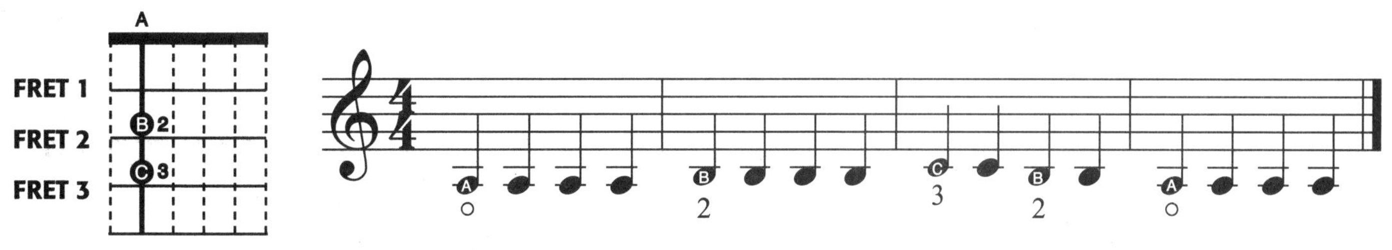

Jamming on 5 and 6

Track 9

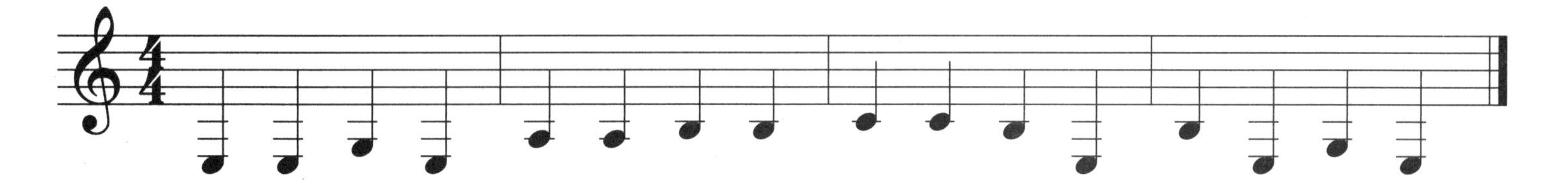

Two-String Rock

Track 10

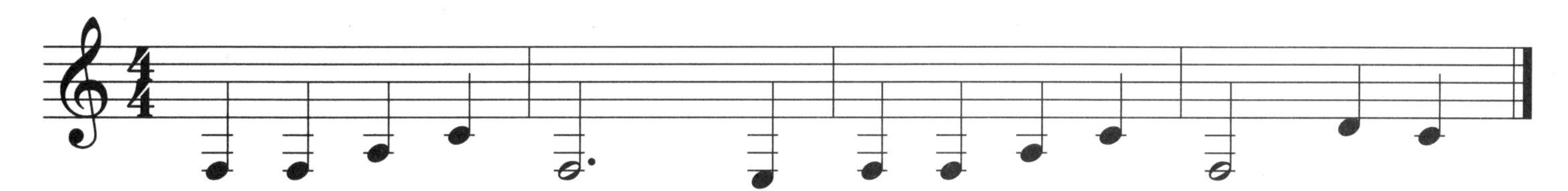

Easy Rock Riffs on the 5th and 6th Strings

Repeat Signs

The double dots inside the double bars are *repeat signs*, and they indicate that everything between the double bars must be repeated.

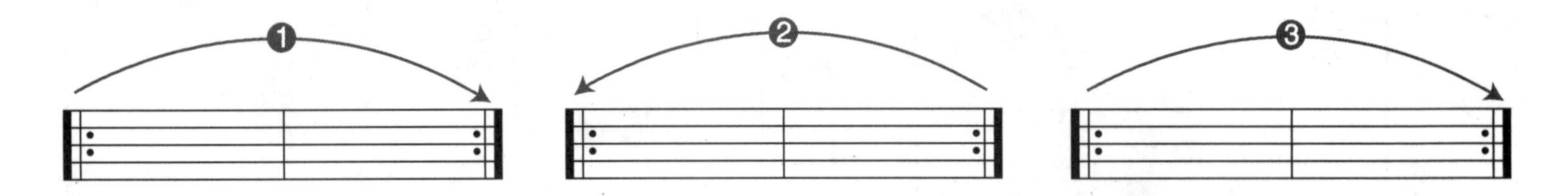

My Generation  Track 11

Released in 1965, "My Generation" by The Who was ranked No. 11 on *Rolling Stone* magazine's list of the 500 Greatest Songs of All Time.

Words and Music by
Peter Townshend

When I Come Around  Track 12

This 1995 Green Day hit was a single from the band's third album, *Dookie*.

Words by Billie Joe
Music by Green Day

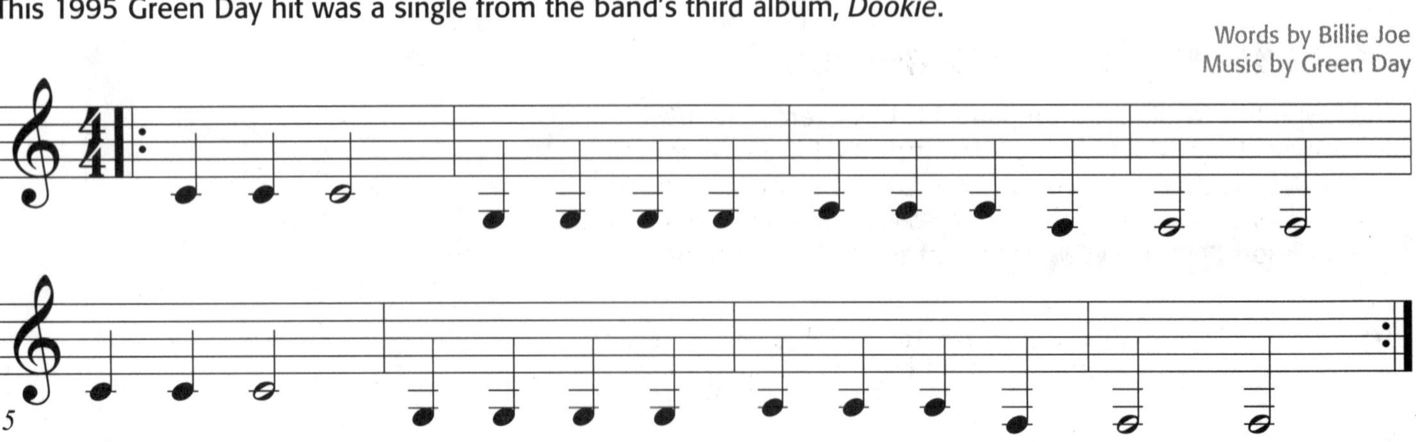

Iron Man Track 13

"Iron Man" was on Black Sabbath's 1970 album, *Paranoid*. Led by singer Ozzy Osbourne, the lineup on this album featured guitarist Tony Iommi.

Words and Music by Frank Iommi, John Osbourne, William Ward and Terence Butler

Hello, I Love You  Track 14

A single from Jim Morrison and The Doors' 1968 album *Waiting for the Sun,* "Hello, I Love You" was a number one hit.

Words and Music by The Doors

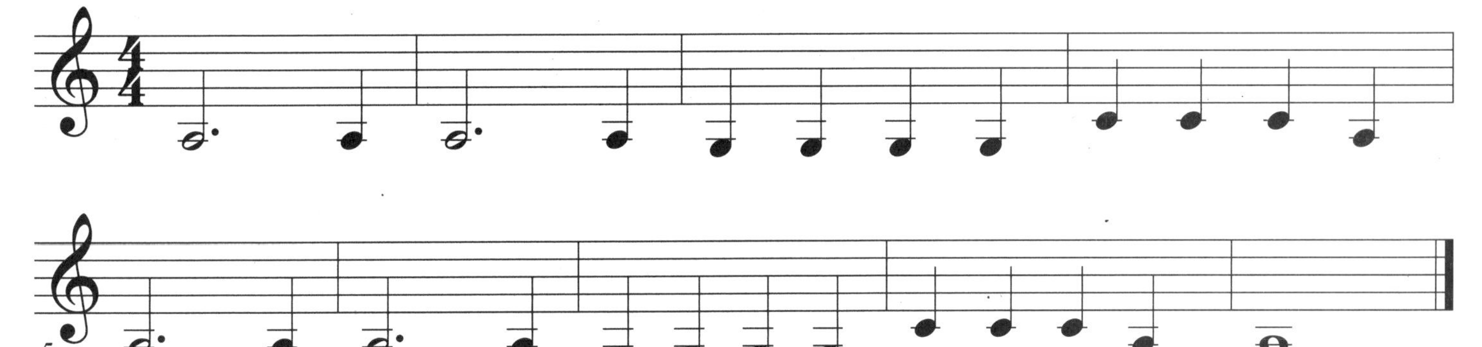

Silent Guitar Calisthenics 3

As with the calisthenics on page 11, this exercise is silent because it involves only the left hand. Do this as slowly as possible, keeping one finger down on the string as you add the other and pressing the string down more firmly than usual. Remember to place the fingers just to the left of the frets.

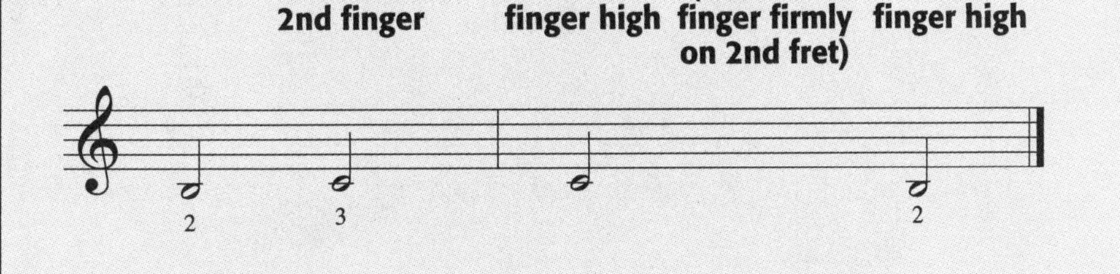

When both fingers are down, they should look similar to this.

The 4th String D

Track 15

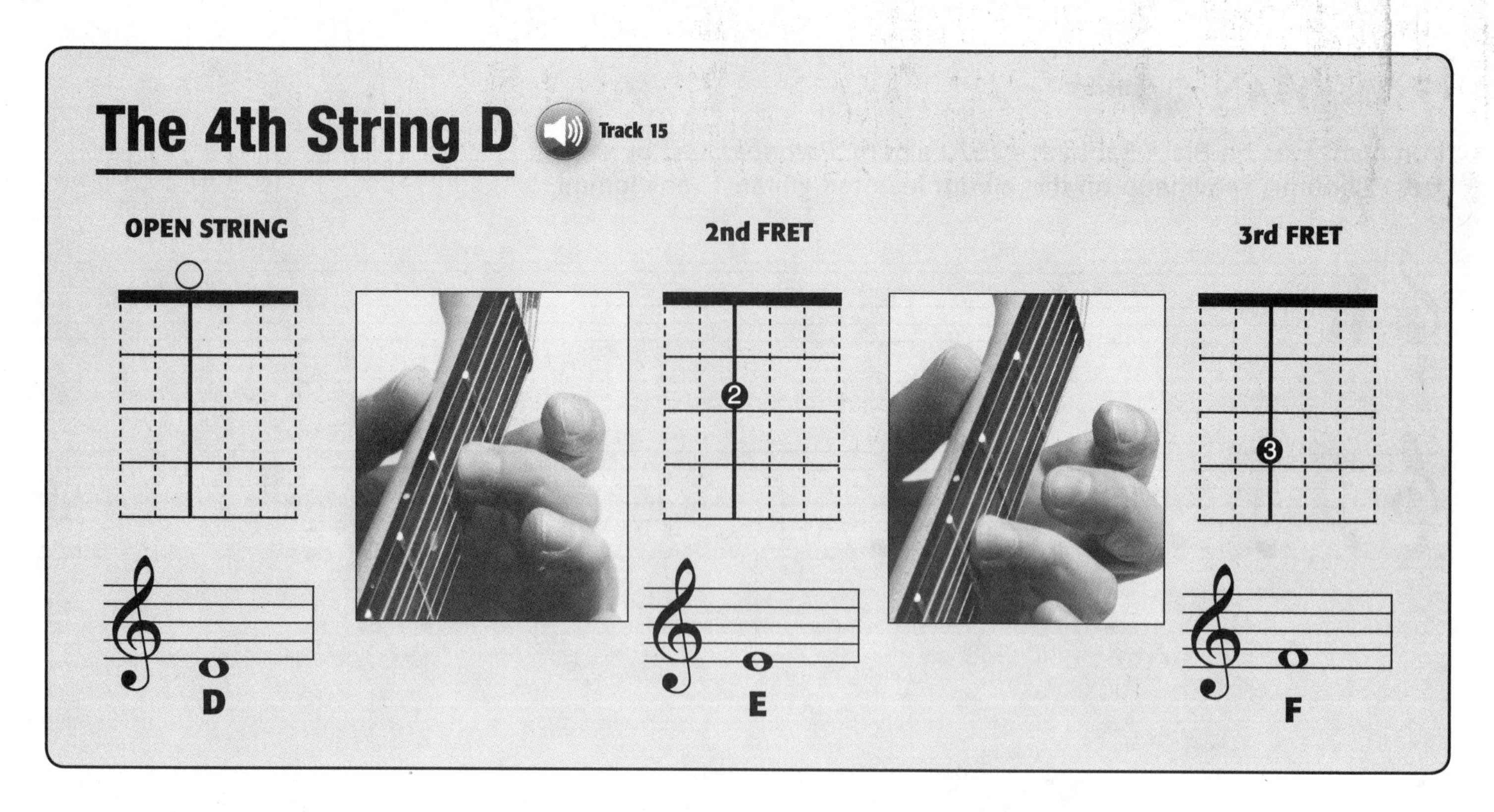

4th-String Riff

Track 16

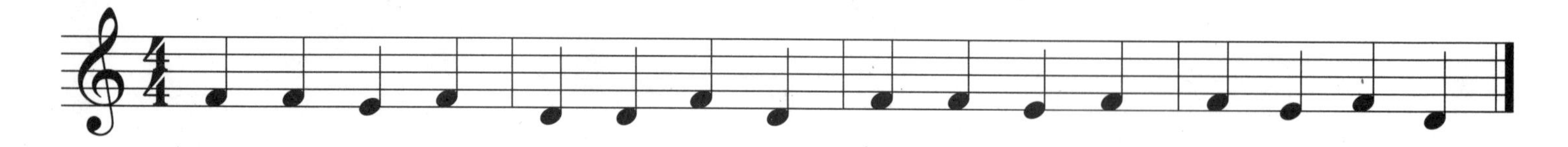

1950s Rock Lick

Track 17

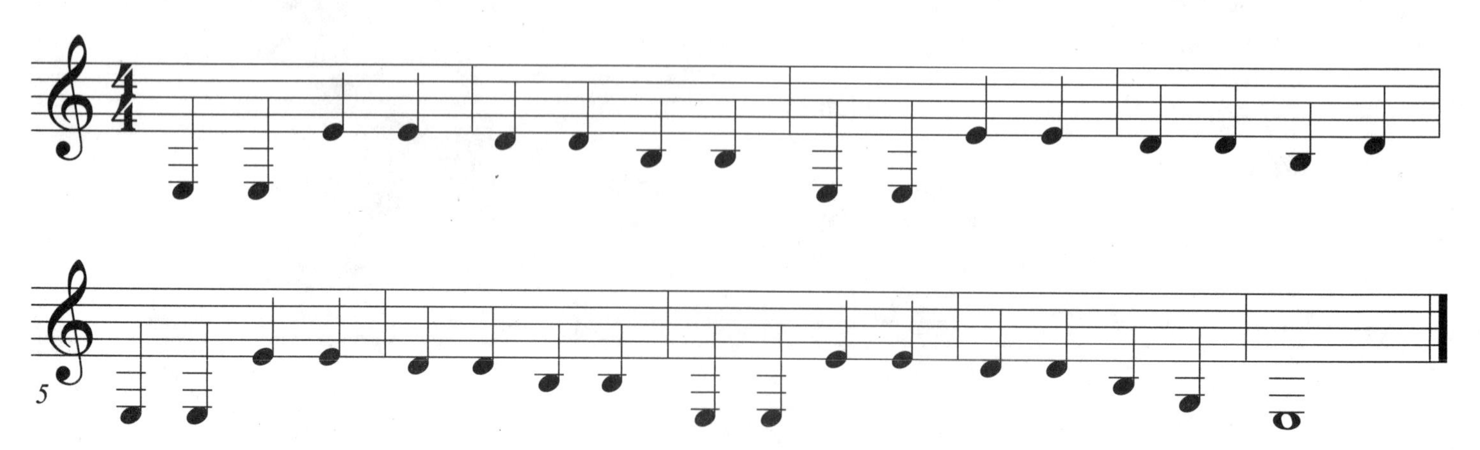

Freeway Jam

Track 18

Jeff Beck's guitar playing, especially on the 1975 album *Blow by Blow*, has been an inspiration to rock guitarists everywhere. "Freeway Jam" was one of the most popular cuts on the album, which was produced by George Martin, sometimes called the "fifth Beatle."

By Max Middleton

Stairway to Heaven

"Stairway to Heaven" by Led Zeppelin is one of the most popular rock songs of all time. This is the bass line for the last verse, after the song's signature guitar solo by Jimmy Page.

Words and Music by
Jimmy Page and Robert Plant

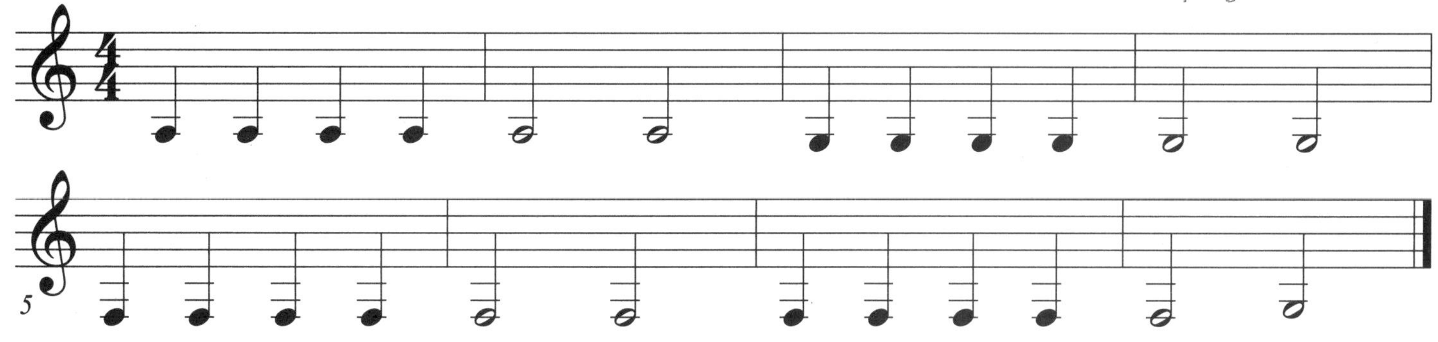

Wild Child

Track 20

This song was on The Doors' album *The Soft Parade*, which was released in 1969.

Words and Music by The Doors

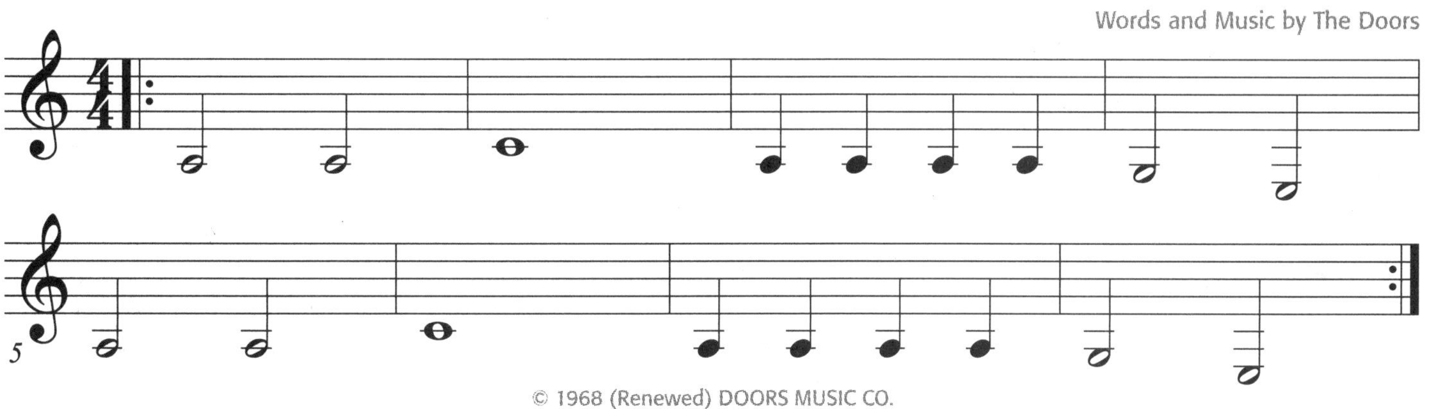

Playing Two Notes Together

Track 21

Until now, you have been playing one note at a time, but in the next example, you will play two notes at once. Make sure to pick the notes quickly so they produce one sound and do not have the effect of two separate notes.

Blues in 3

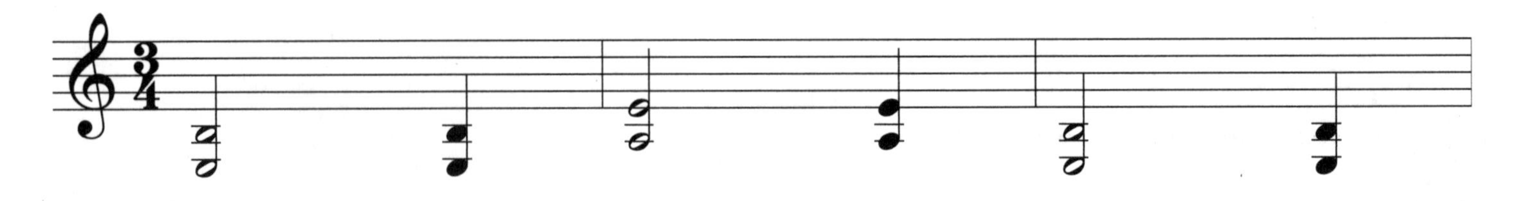

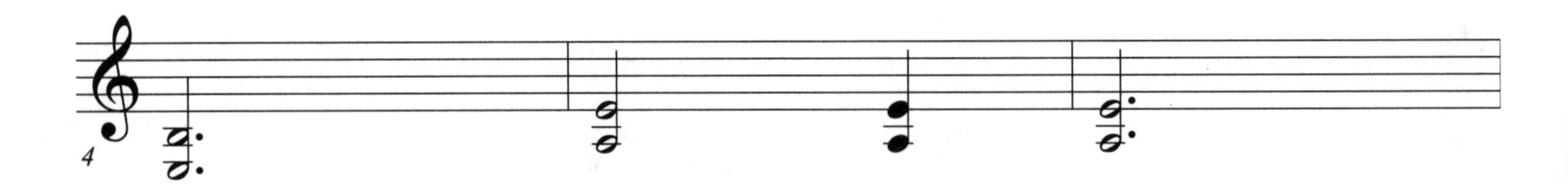

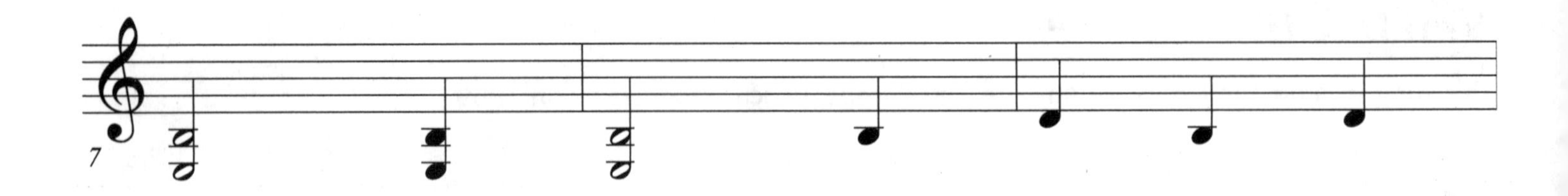

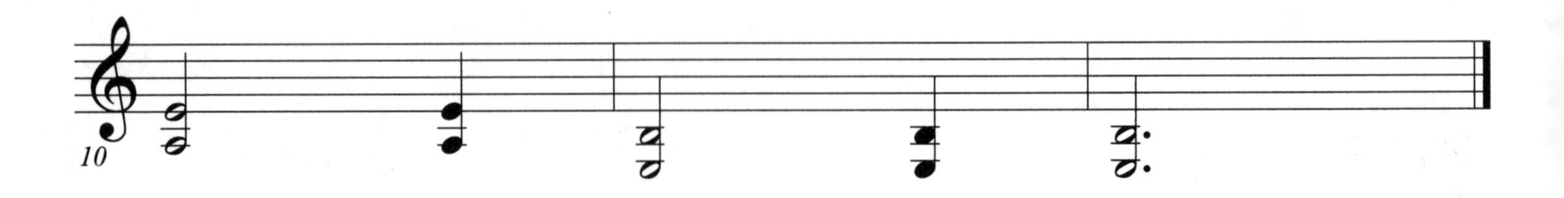

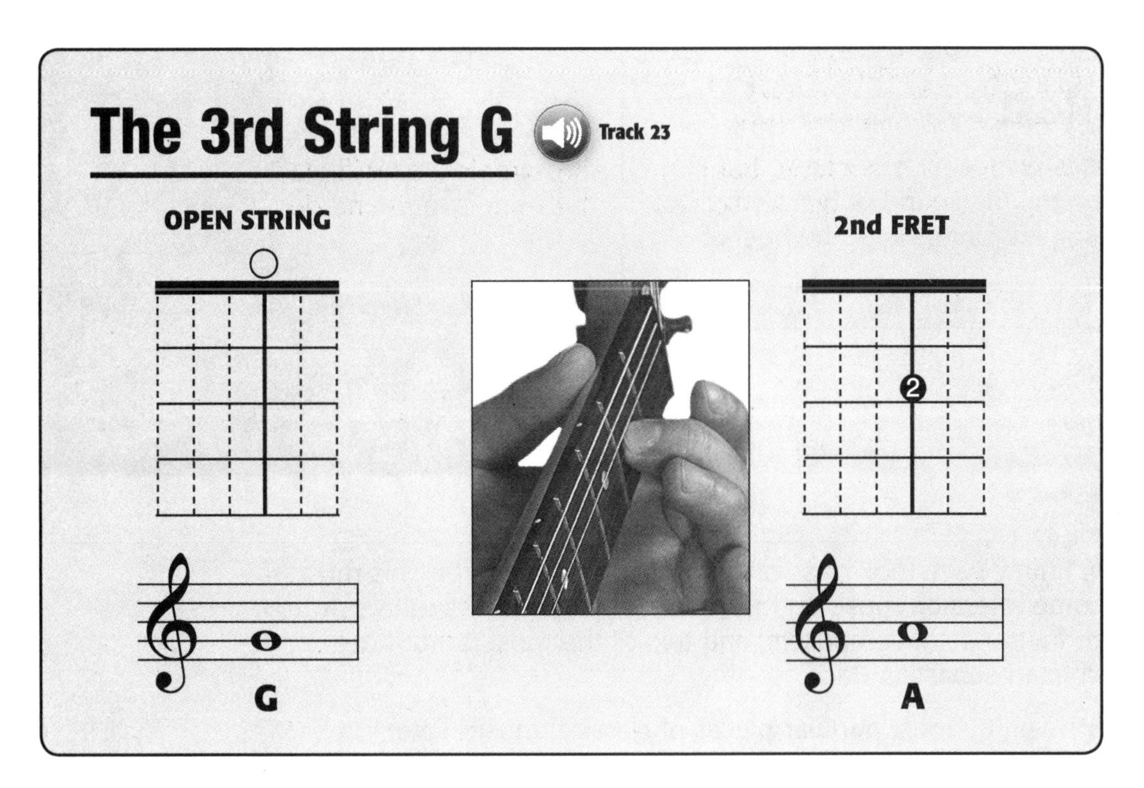

JUMPIN' JACK FLASH

Track 24

This song was a hit for The Rolling Stones in 1968.

Words and Music by
Mick Jagger and Keith Richards

Quarter Rest

This sign indicates silence for one count. To accomplish this, stop the sound of the strings by lightly touching the strings with the heel of your right hand.

Ode to Joy  Track 25

Before forming Led Zeppelin, Jimmy Page took classical guitar lessons to improve his music-reading skills in order to become a session musician in recording studios. Classical music spans hundreds of years and thousands of composers, and two of the most famous are Ludwig van Beethoven and Johann Sebastian Bach.

Beethoven's "Ode to Joy" is one of the most popular pieces of classical music. Later, on page 54, you will learn a tune based on Bach's music, which Jimmy admired considering he plays Bach's "Bouree in E Minor" during "Heartbreaker" on the Led Zeppelin live album *How the West Was Won*.

Rockabilly Sound  Track 26

Power Chords

A *chord* is technically three or more notes played together, but when you see symbols like A5, D5, or E5, these are special two-note chords called *power chords*. Add some distortion, play them loud, and you will hear how they got their name and why they are some of the most important chords in rock.

Three-Chord Progression

Higher

From Creed's 1999 album *Human Clay,* "Higher" was a breakthrough hit for the band, peaking at No. 7 on *Billboard's* Hot 100 chart.

Words and Music by Mark Tremonti and Scott Stapp

Rock Duet

Track 29

This song is a *duet*, which is a piece written for two performers. You can play either the first or second part here, and have a teacher or friend play the other part. Do this with all of the duets in this book.

Blitzkrieg Bop  Track 30

This song was released as the Ramones' debut single in February 1976.

Words and Music by
Jeffrey Hyman, John Cummings,
Douglas Colvin and Thomas Erdelyi

The 2nd String B

Track 31

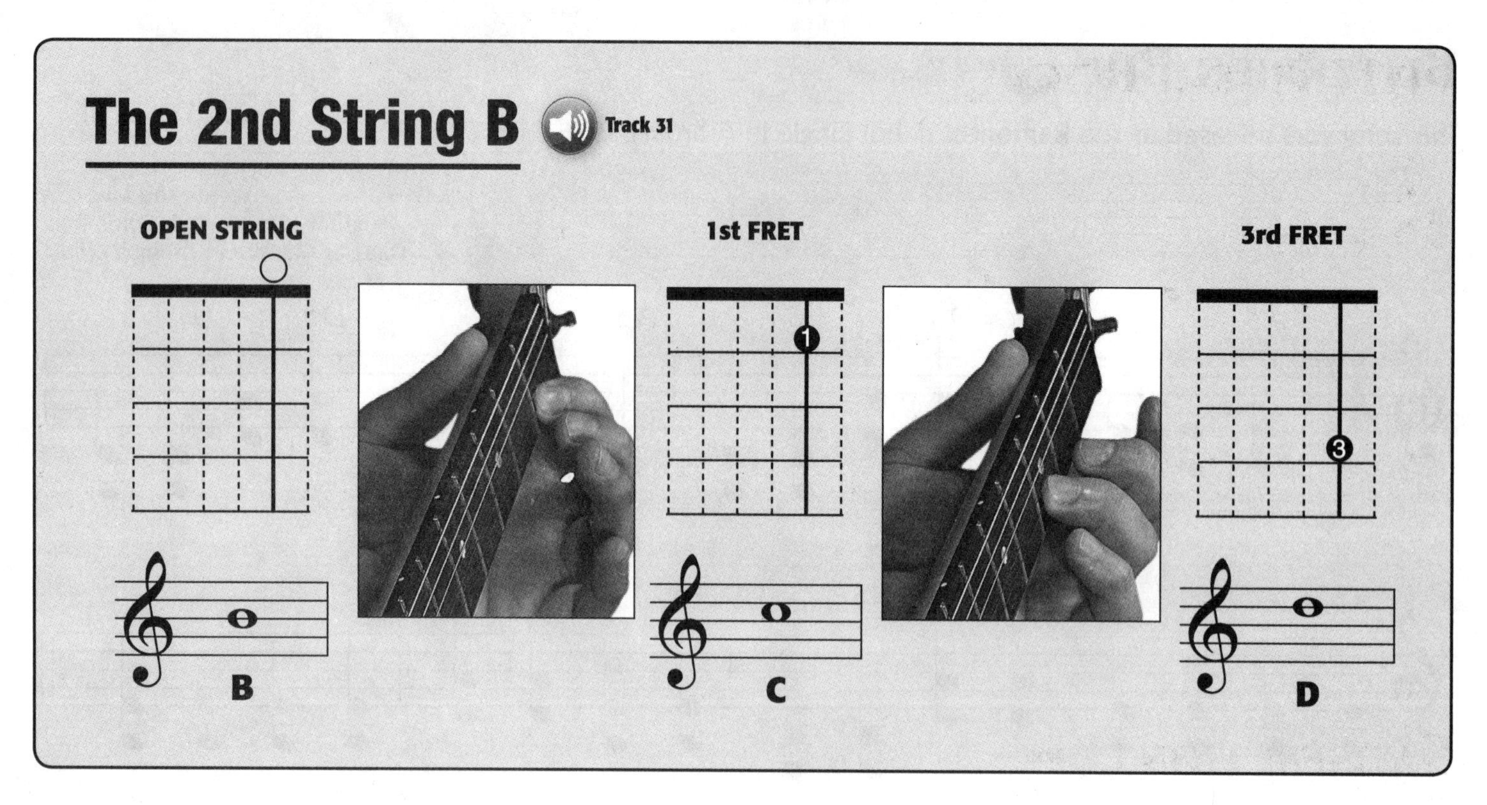

Classic Rock Lick

Track 32

Five-String Rock Track 33

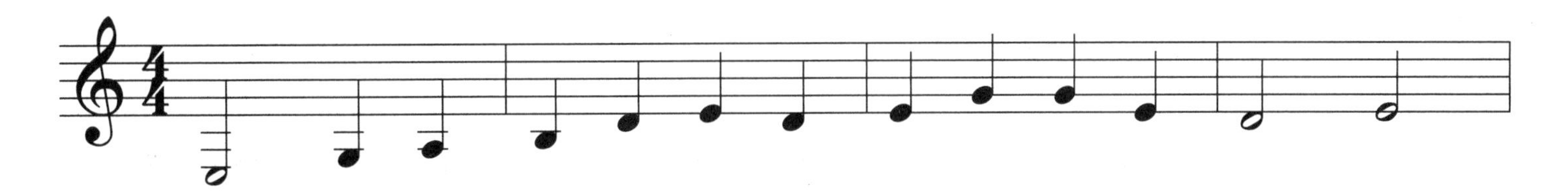

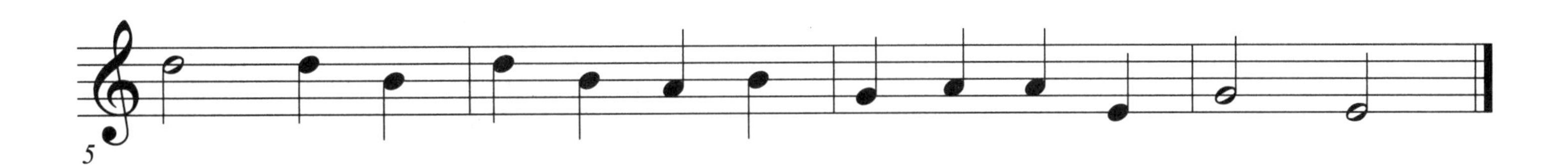

Satisfaction Track 34

This song, released in 1965, was The Rolling Stones' first hit in the United States.

Words and Music by
Mick Jagger and Keith Richards

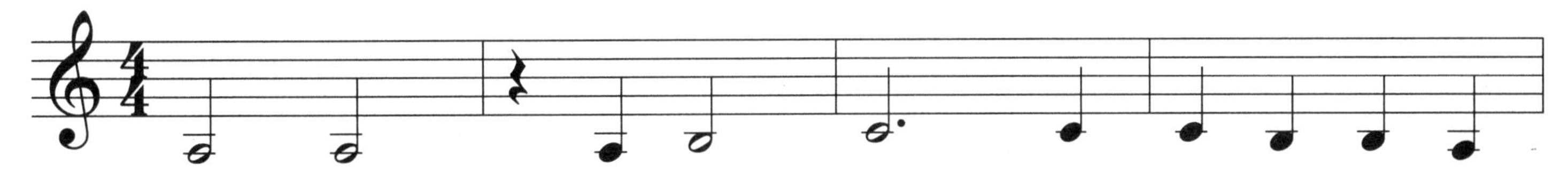

Rise Above This Track 35

A big hit for Seether in 2008, "Rise Above This" was a single from the band's album *Finding Beauty in Negative Spaces*.

Music and Lyrics by
Shaun Morgan, Dale Stewart
and John Humphrey

The 1st String E

Track 37

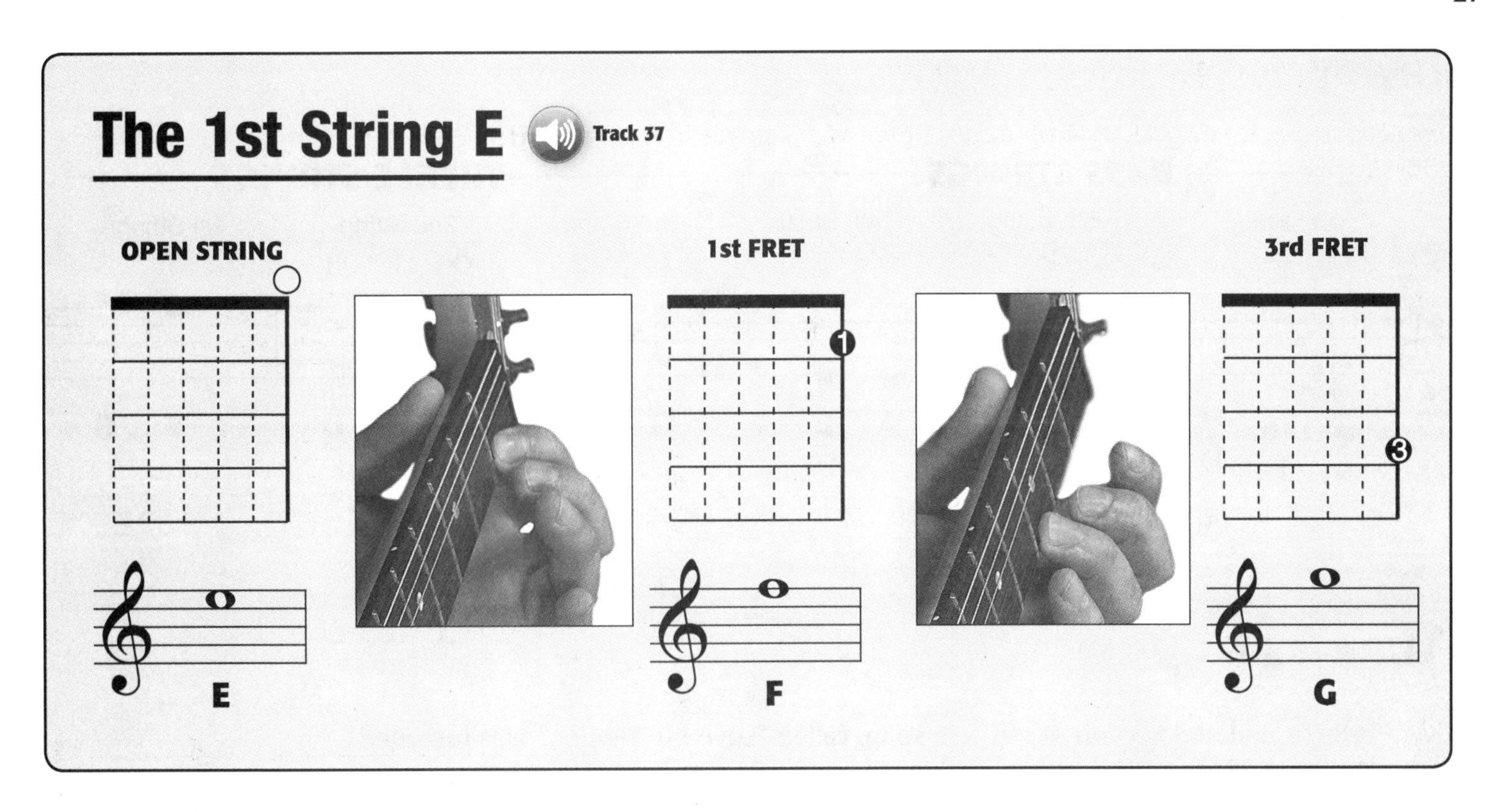

Jamming with E, F, and G

Track 38

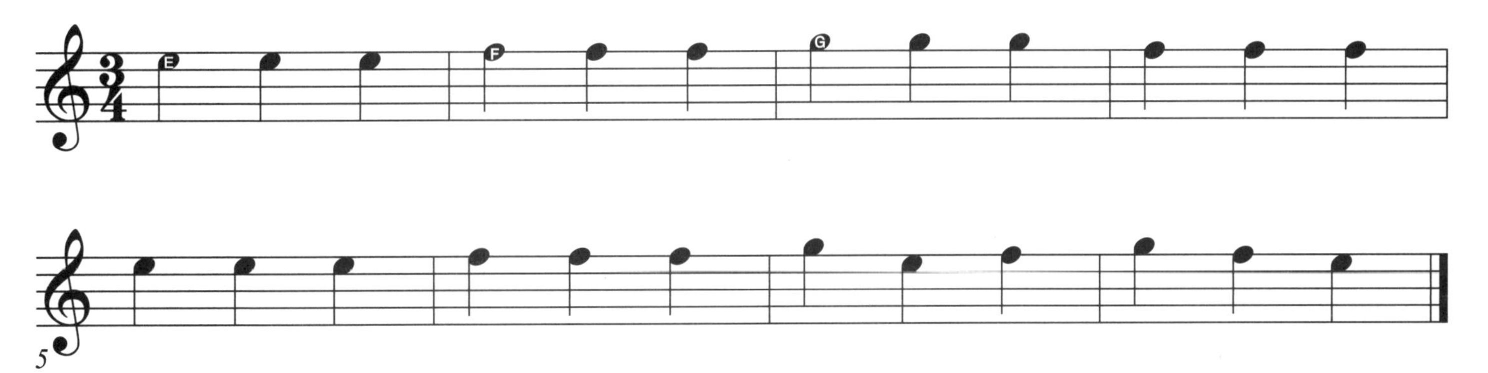

Review

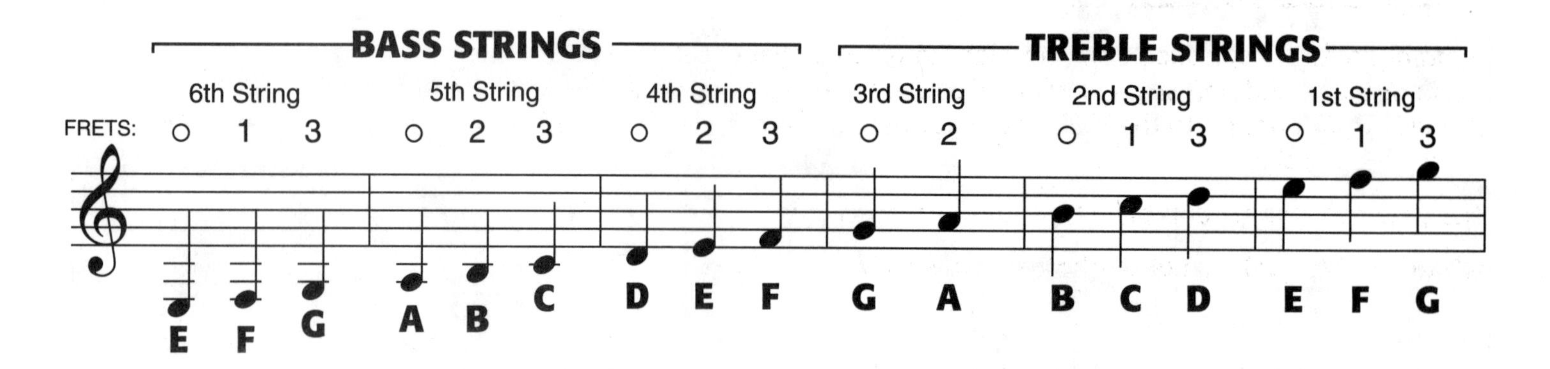

AURA LEE

Track 39

Elvis Presley's updated version of this folk song, called "Love Me Tender," was recorded and released in 1956.

The Major Scale

A *major scale* is a specific pattern of eight tones in alphabetical order. The pattern of *whole steps* and *half steps* is what gives the major scale its distinct sound. The distance from one fret to the next fret, up or down, is a half step. Two half steps make a whole step.

The pattern of whole and half steps for a major scale is:

whole–whole–half–whole–whole–whole–half

The highest note of the scale, having the same letter name as the first note, is called the *octave* note.

OCTAVE NOTE

C D E F G A B C

WHOLE STEP WHOLE STEP HALF STEP WHOLE STEP WHOLE STEP WHOLE STEP HALF STEP

C Major Scale

It is easy to visualize whole steps and half steps on a piano keyboard. Notice there are whole steps between every white-key note except E–F and B–C.

Whole steps—One key between

Half steps—No key between

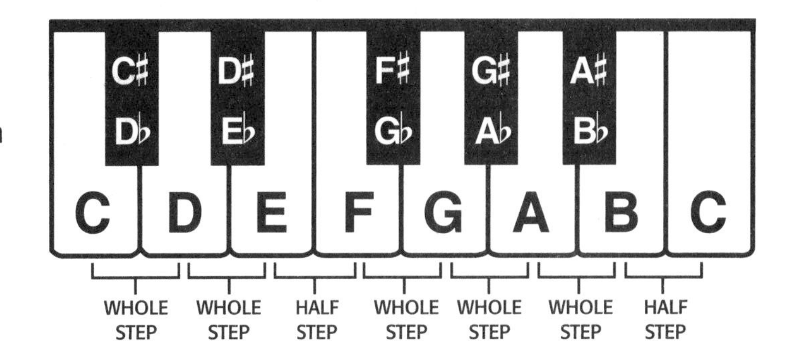

C Major Scale Exercise Track 40

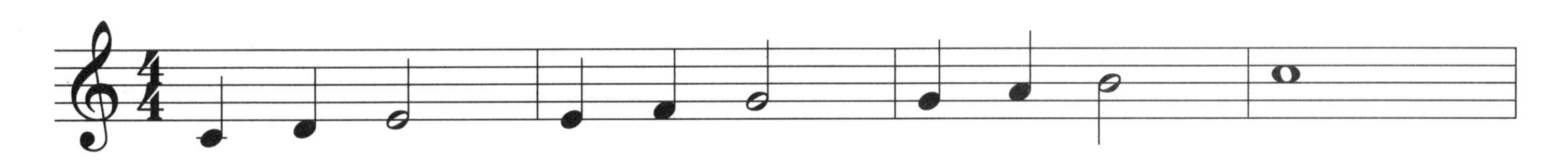

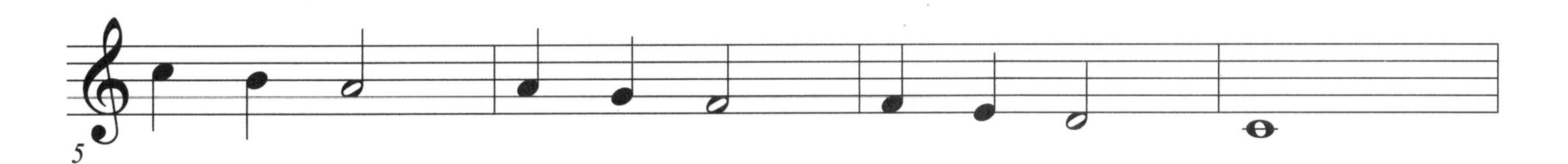

Six-String Em Chord

The lowercase "m" means *minor*. We think of minor chords as having a sad, serious sound.

NOTE: A chord name like C, without an "m" after the letter name, indicates a major chord, which has a happier, brighter sound.

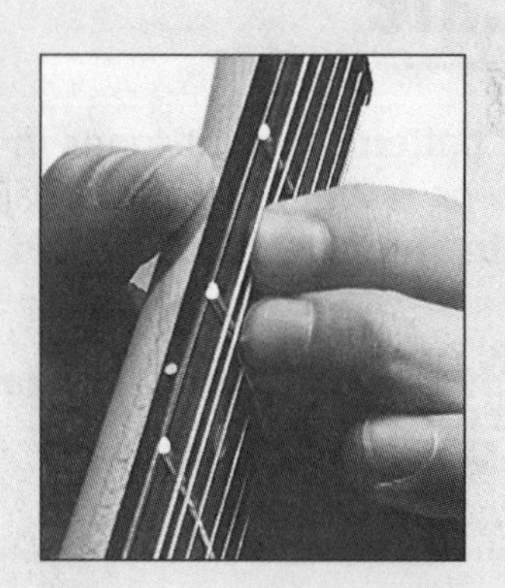

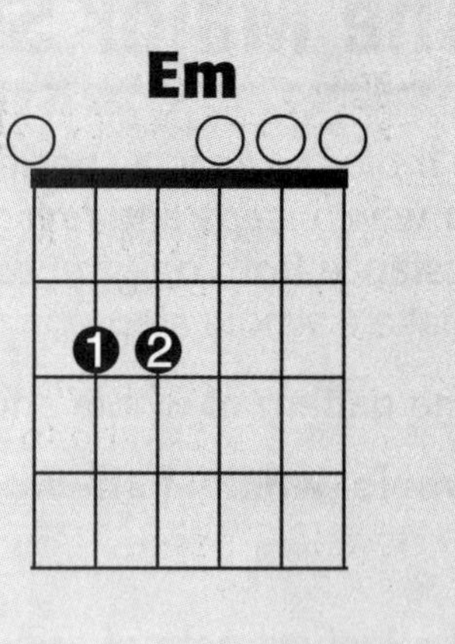

To play this chord, place your 1st and 2nd fingers on the 2nd fret of the 5th and 4th strings and strum all six strings. This chord can also be played with your 2nd and 3rd fingers.

You learned to strum back on page 6. Since then, you have been strumming two-string power chords. On this page, you will be strumming a full six-string Em chord. The "m" in Em stands for "minor," so when you see "Em," you say "E Minor."

Quarter-Note Slash

Instead of using notes, sometimes chords are notated with slashes. A *quarter-note slash* tells you to play a chord for one count. If there is more than one quarter-note slash in a row, the chord symbol above the first note is played for each slash. In this example, the Em chord is played four times.

Play four measures of the Em chord in the example below. Count out loud and keep the rhythm even. Strum firmly and directly downward across the strings to produce a nice, full sound.

Em Strumming Exercise 

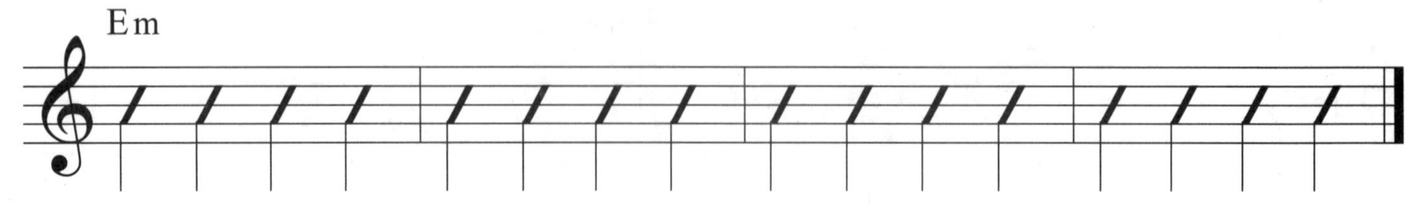

COUNT: 1 & 2 & 3 & 4 & ETC.

Five-String A7 Chord

Some sheet music will use an X in a chord frame to show a string not played, but other music will show a dashed line. This book uses both.

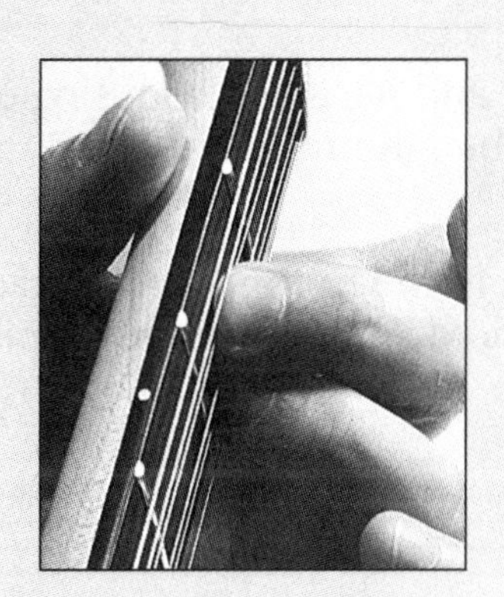

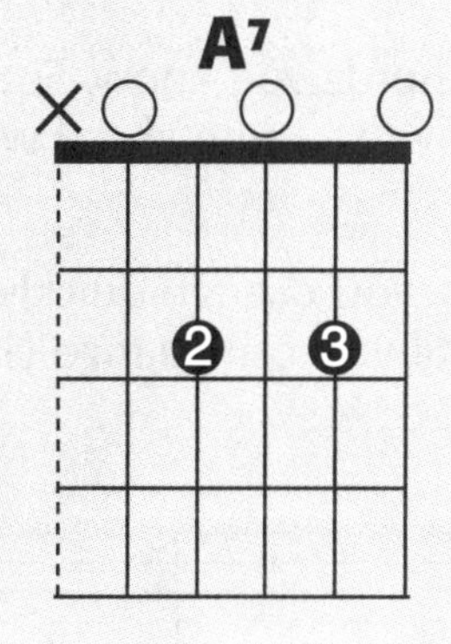

To play the A7 chord, Place your 2nd and 3rd fingers on the 2nd fret of the 4th and 2nd strings, respectively, and only strum from the 5th to the 1st string. Unlike the six-string Em chord, you will not play the 6th string here.

The "7" in A7 stands for "seventh," so when you see "A7," you say either "A Seventh," or "A Seven."

Play four measures of the A7 chord. Count out loud and keep the rhythm even. Remember to strum firmly and directly downward across the strings to produce a nice, full sound.

Strumming the A7 Chord

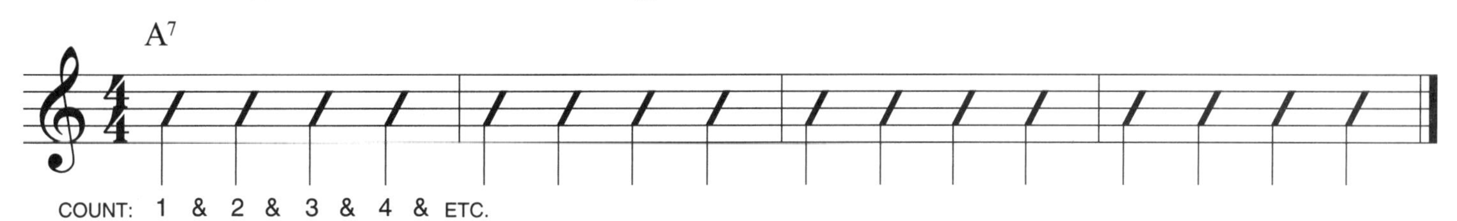

In the example below, you will be changing chords in each measure. Since both the Em and A7 chords are played using the 2nd finger on the 4th string at the 2nd fret, you only need to lift the 3rd finger and place the 1st finger.

Play it slowly at first, and lift and place the two fingers smoothly at exactly the same time as you change chords. Gradually increase the speed as you become more comfortable changing chords.

Strumming Em and A7 Chords

Minor Two-Chord Rock

Track 44

This tune uses the two chords you know, Em and A7, along with single notes and rests. When there are rests, play the same chord when the music resumes until a new chord symbol appears.

In the last two measures, you change quickly from Em to A7 and back. Practice just those two measures slowly until you can change chords in time, and then play the entire tune.

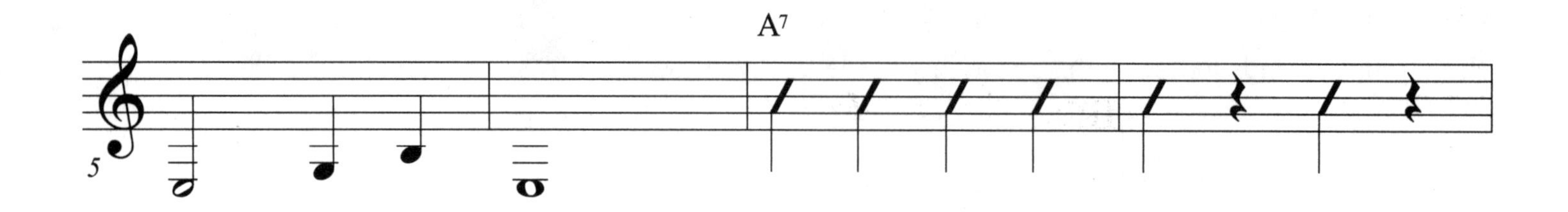

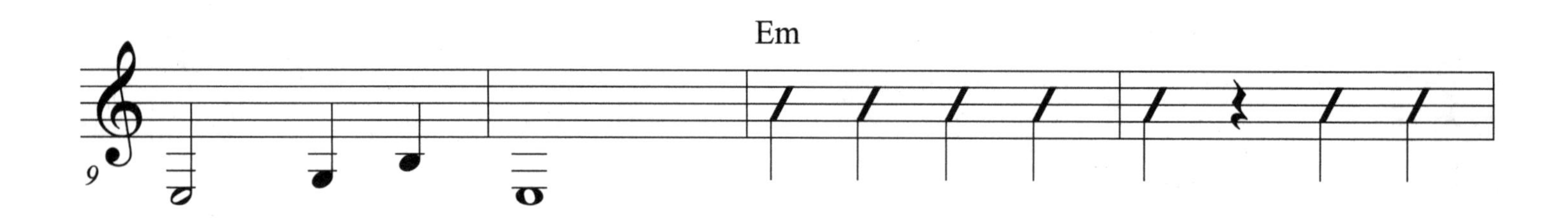

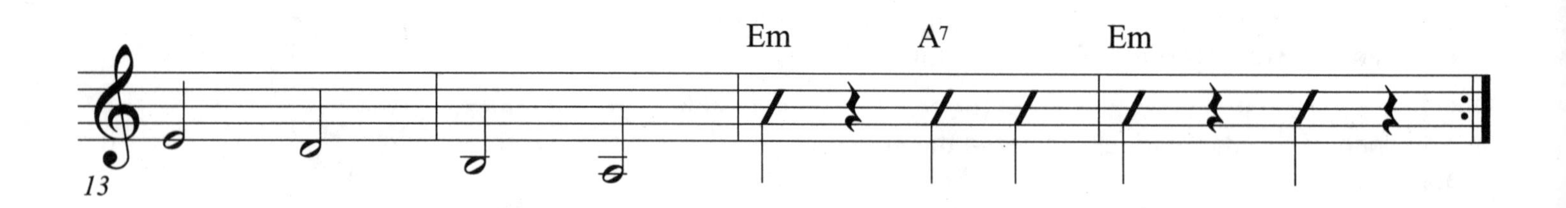

Introducing High A

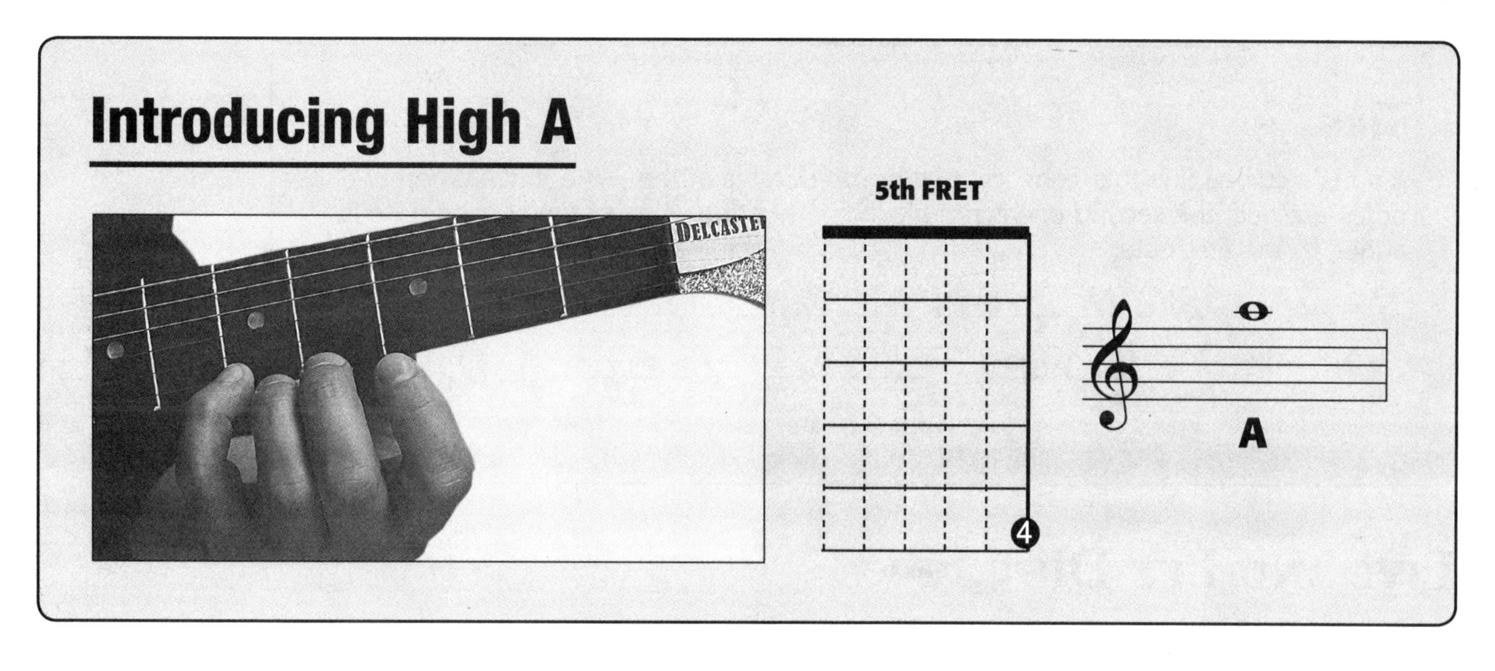

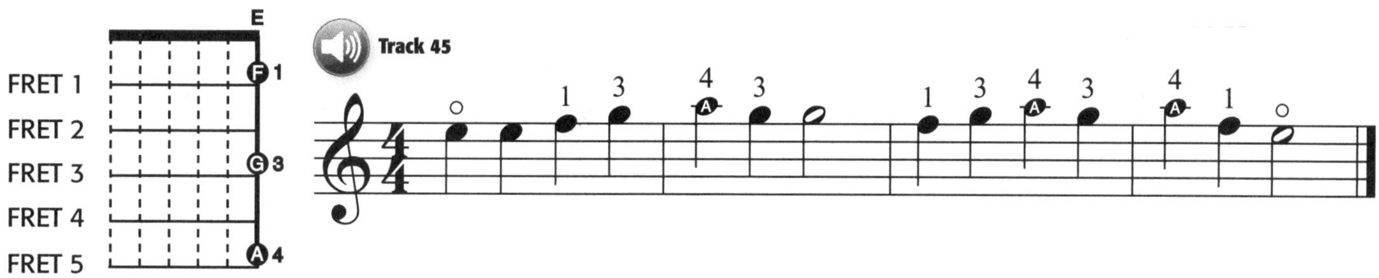

Rockin' in Dorian Mode

Track 46

A *mode* is a type of scale that uses the notes of another scale, such as the major scale (page 29), in a different order. The *Dorian mode* uses the notes of the C Major scale starting on D instead of C.

Ties

A *tie* is a curved line that connects two or more notes of the same pitch. When two notes are tied, the second one is not played; rather, the value of the second note is added to the first note.

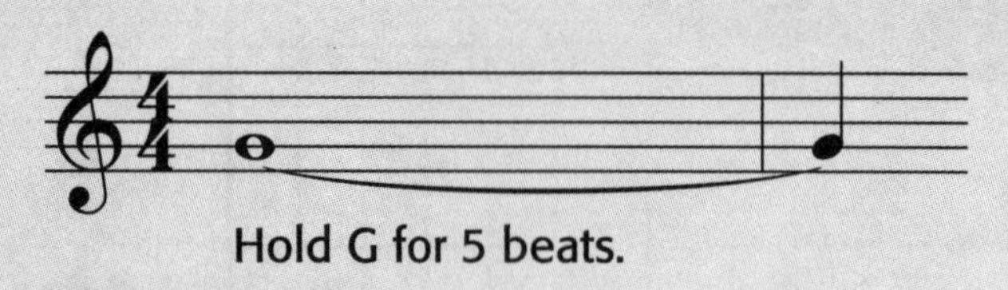

Hold G for 5 beats.

Live and Let Die  Track 47

Written specifically for the James Bond movie of the same name, "Live and Let Die" was a huge hit for Paul McCartney and Wings in 1973.

Words and Music by
Paul McCartney and Linda McCartney

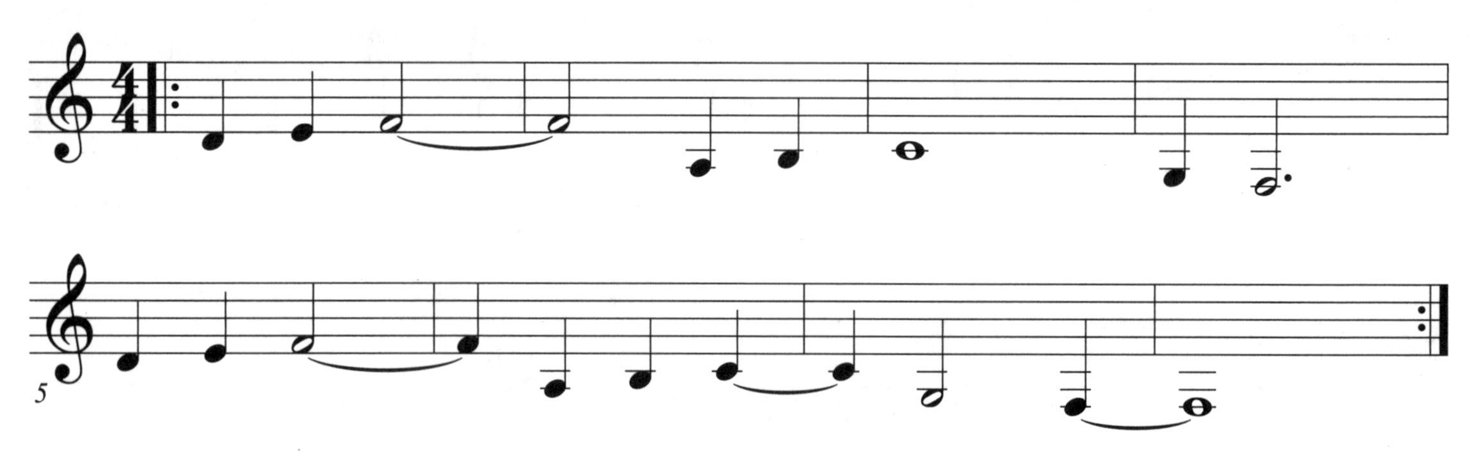

Stairway to Heaven (Lead Guitar Solo)  Track 48

Jimmy Page played one of the most-admired lead guitar solos in rock history in this famous song.

Words and Music by
Jimmy Page and Robert Plant

Eighth Notes

Eighth notes are black notes with a flag added to the stem: ♪ or ♪.

Two or more eighth notes are written with beams: ♫ or ♫, ♫♫ or ♫♫.
Each eighth note receives half a beat.

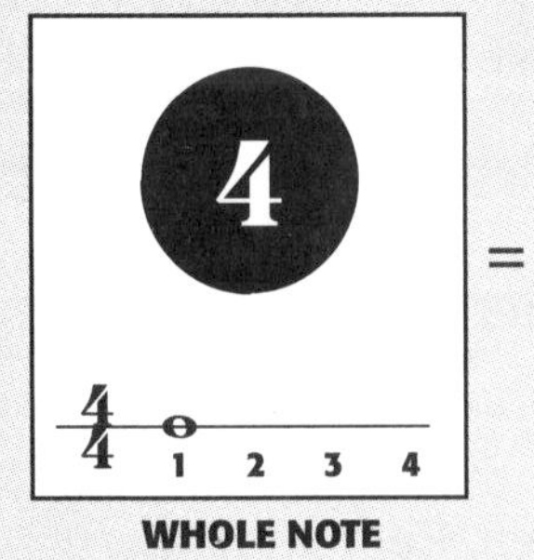

WHOLE NOTE

=

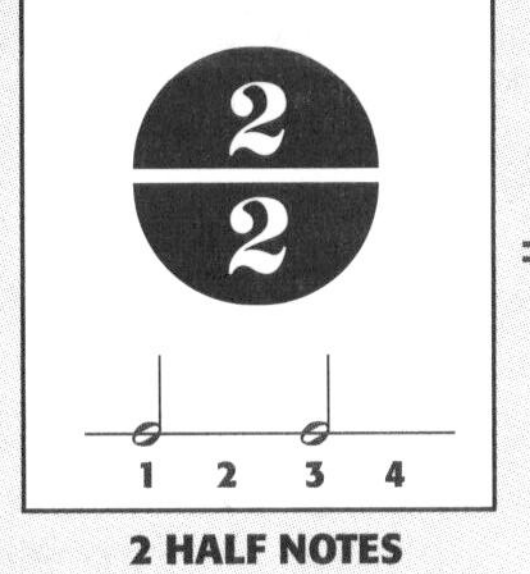

2 HALF NOTES

=

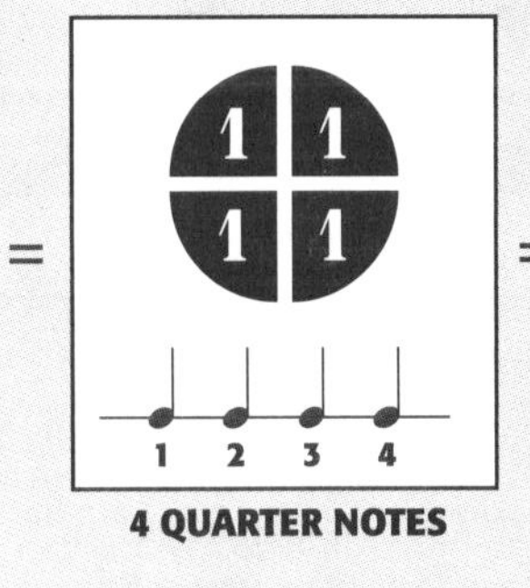

4 QUARTER NOTES

=

8 EIGHTH NOTES

Use alternating down-strokes ⊓ and *up-strokes* V, picking up towards ceiling, on eighth notes.

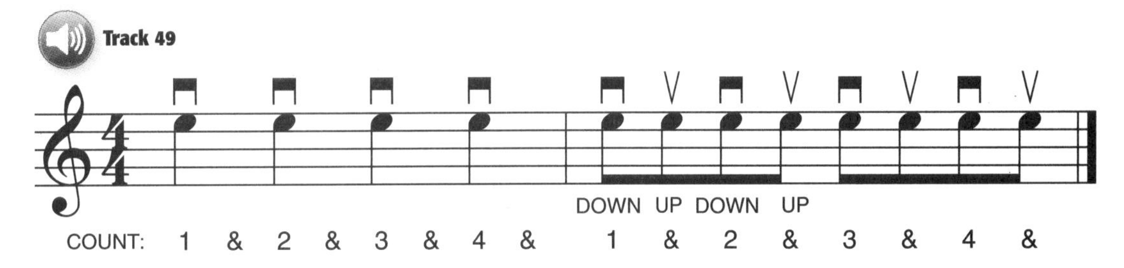

Eighth-Note Exercise

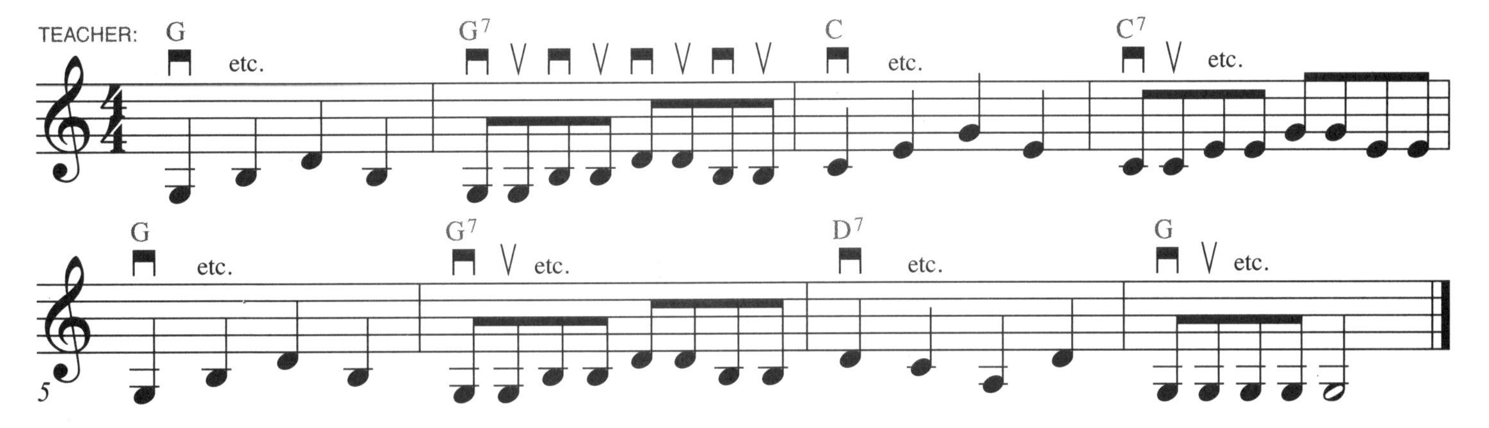

IMMIGRANT SONG

One of Led Zeppelin's top radio hits, this song was on their 1970 album *Led Zeppelin III*.

Words and Music by
Jimmy Page and Robert Plant

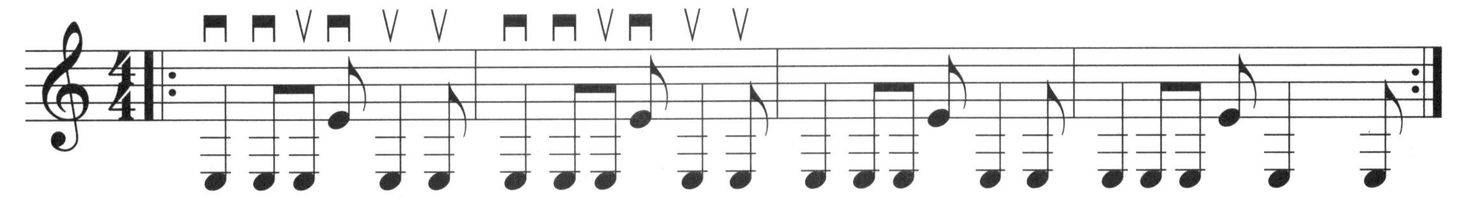

Four-String D7 Chord

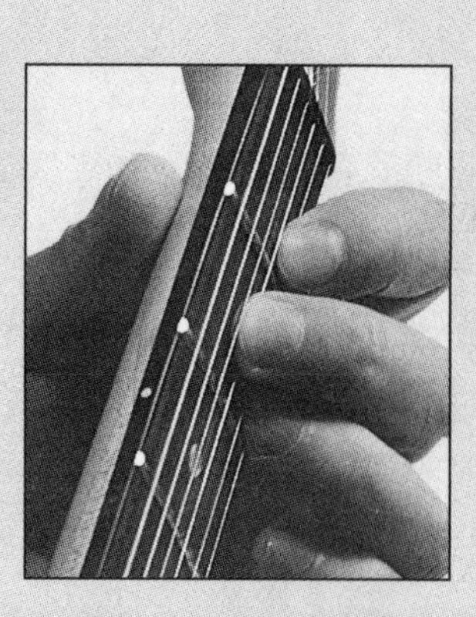

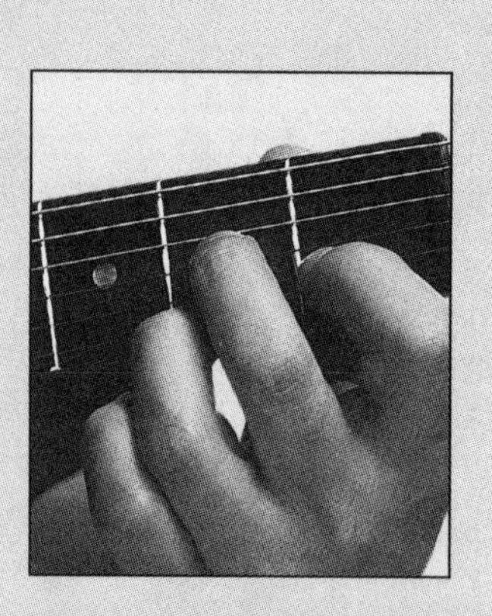

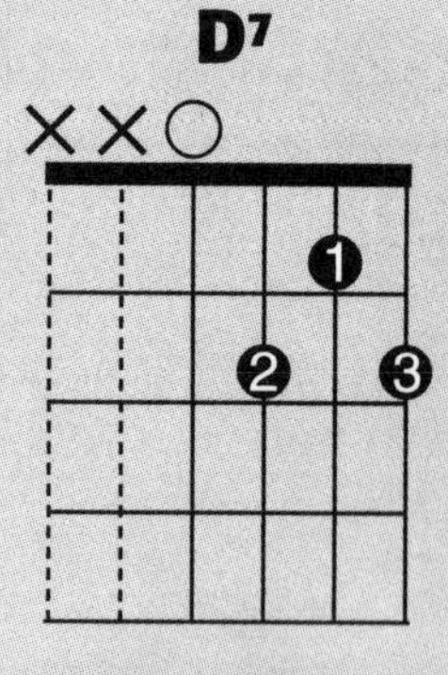

The four-string D7 chord uses three fingers. Place your 1st finger on the 1st fret of the 2nd string, and your 2nd and 3rd fingers on the 2nd fret of the 3rd and 1st strings. Only strum the 4th through 1st strings. Do not strum the 5th or 6th strings.

Play four measures of the D7 chord. Count out loud and keep the rhythm even. Remember to strum firmly and directly downward across the strings to produce a nice full sound.

Remember to practice the changes slowly, and then gradually increase the speed as you become more comfortable changing chords.

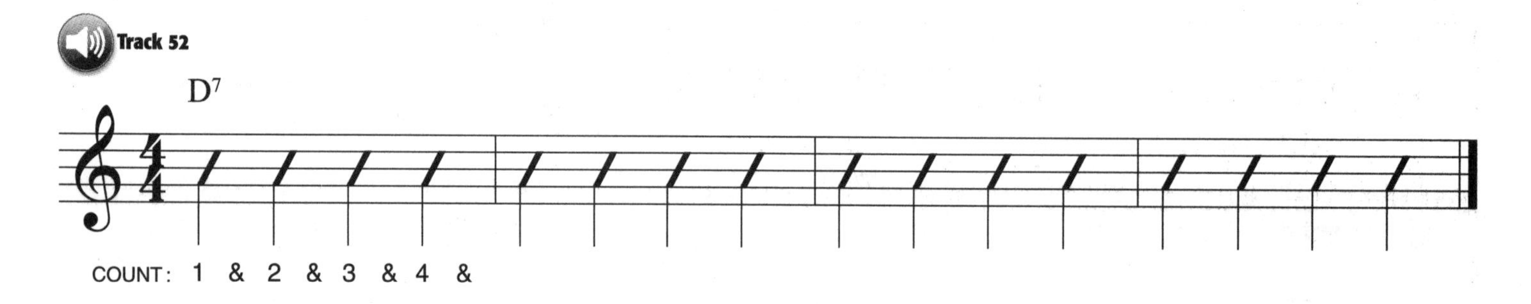

D7 and A7 Chord Exercise

Track 53

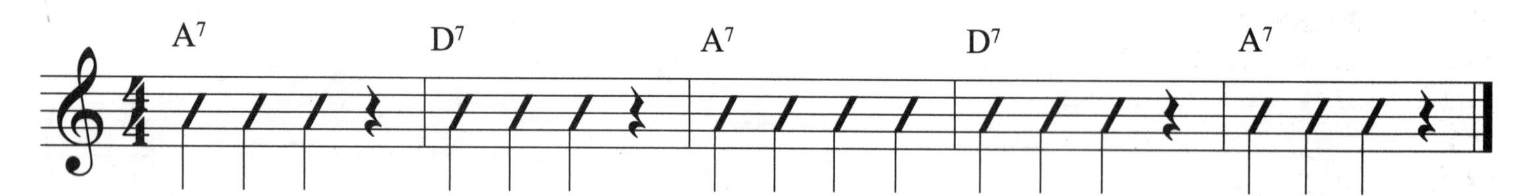

D7 Chord with Notes

This example combines single notes with the D7 chord.

Six-String E Chord

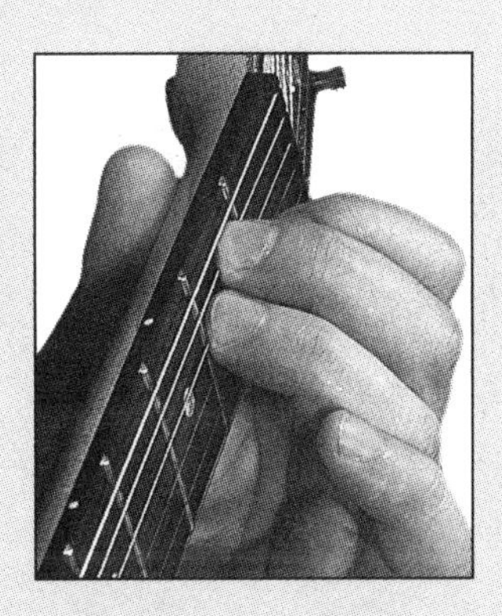

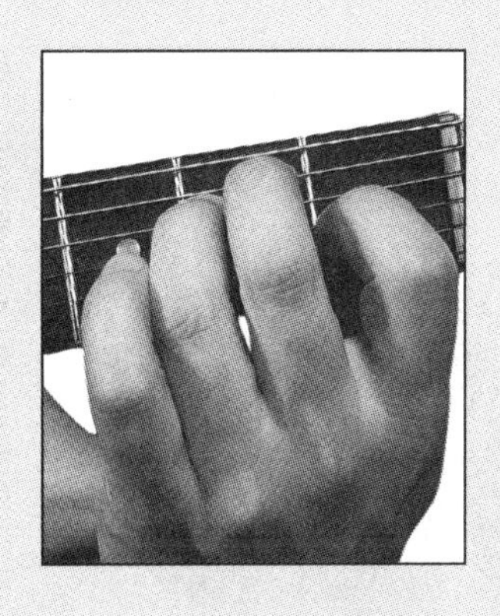

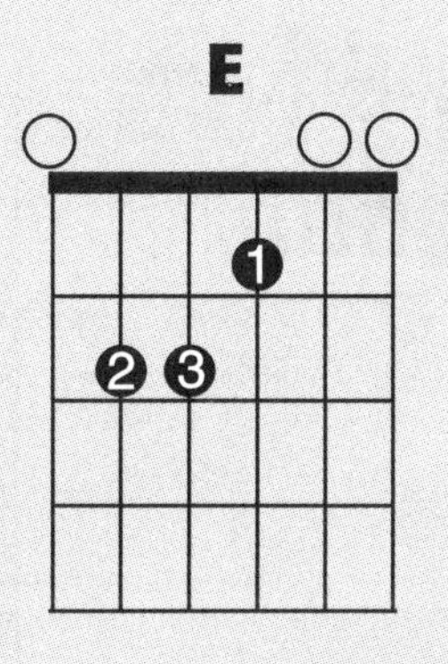

This chord also uses three fingers. Place your 1st finger on the 1st fret of the 3rd string, and your 2nd and 3rd fingers on the 2nd fret of the 5th and 4th strings. Strum all six strings.

The six-string E chord is a major chord. We learned on page 30 that when the chord name is just a letter, such as "E," it is a major chord. The E Minor chord we already learned sounds dark or sad, but the E Major chord sounds bright or happy.

Introducing the Eighth-Note Slash

Like an eighth note, the *eighth-note slash* lasts for one half beat. Two or more eighth-note slashes are written with beams.

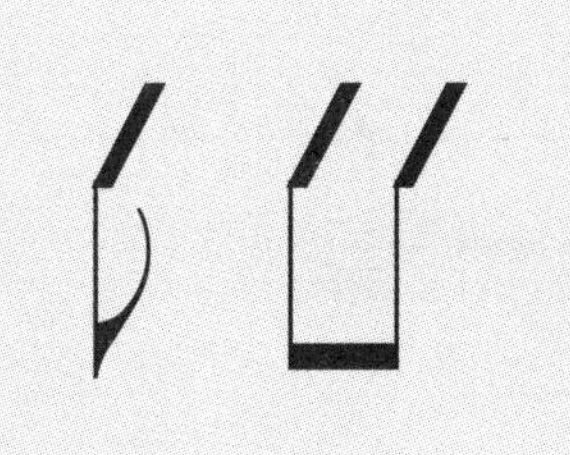

Eighth-Note Slash Exercise

This exercise uses the E and A7 chords with quarter- and eighth-note slashes.

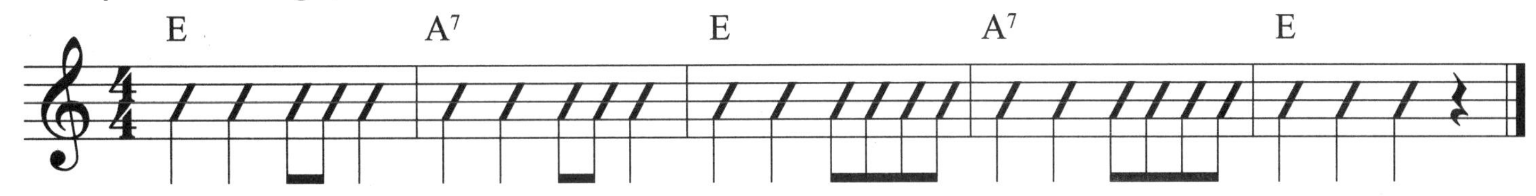

Strumming Exercise with E Chord

Track 56

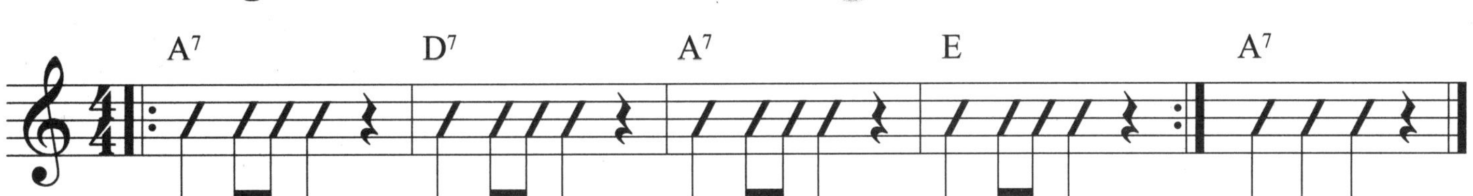

Five-String A Chord

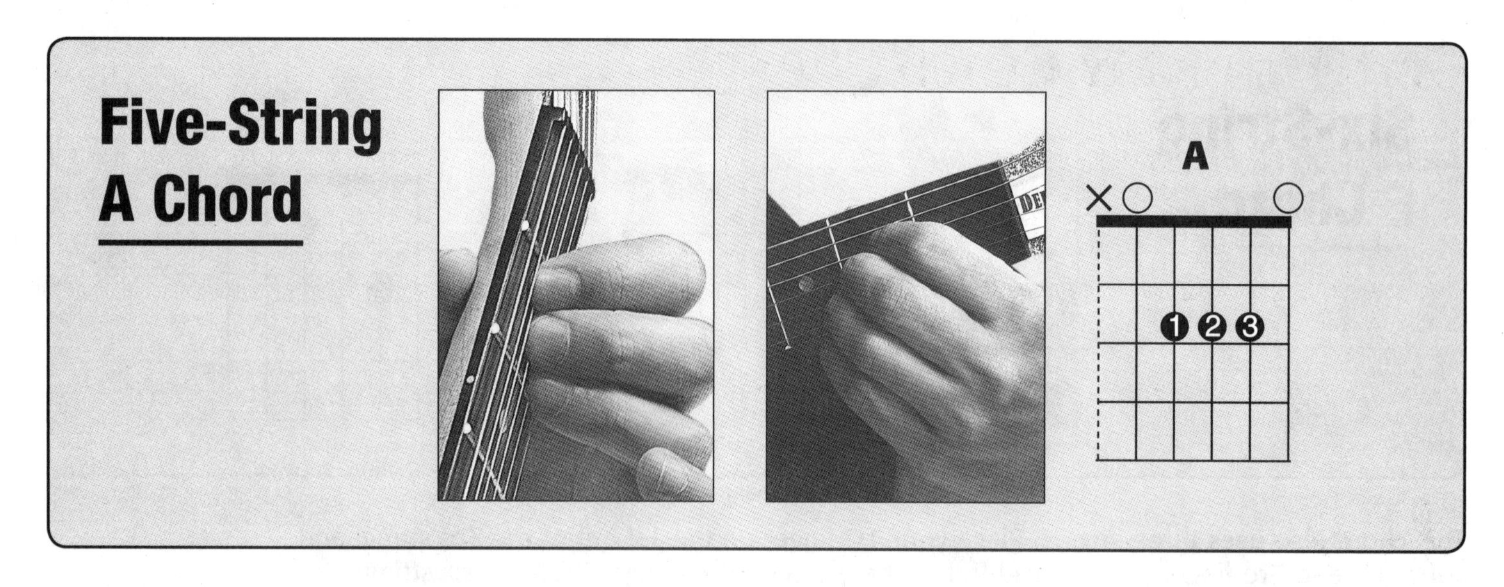

The five-string A chord, or A Major chord, uses three fingers. Place your 1st, 2nd, and 3rd fingers on the 2nd fret of the 4th, 3rd, and 2nd strings. Strum only the 5th to 1st strings.

This example combines the A chord with the D7 chord you learned on page 36. Remember to strum firmly and directly downward across the strings to produce a nice full sound.

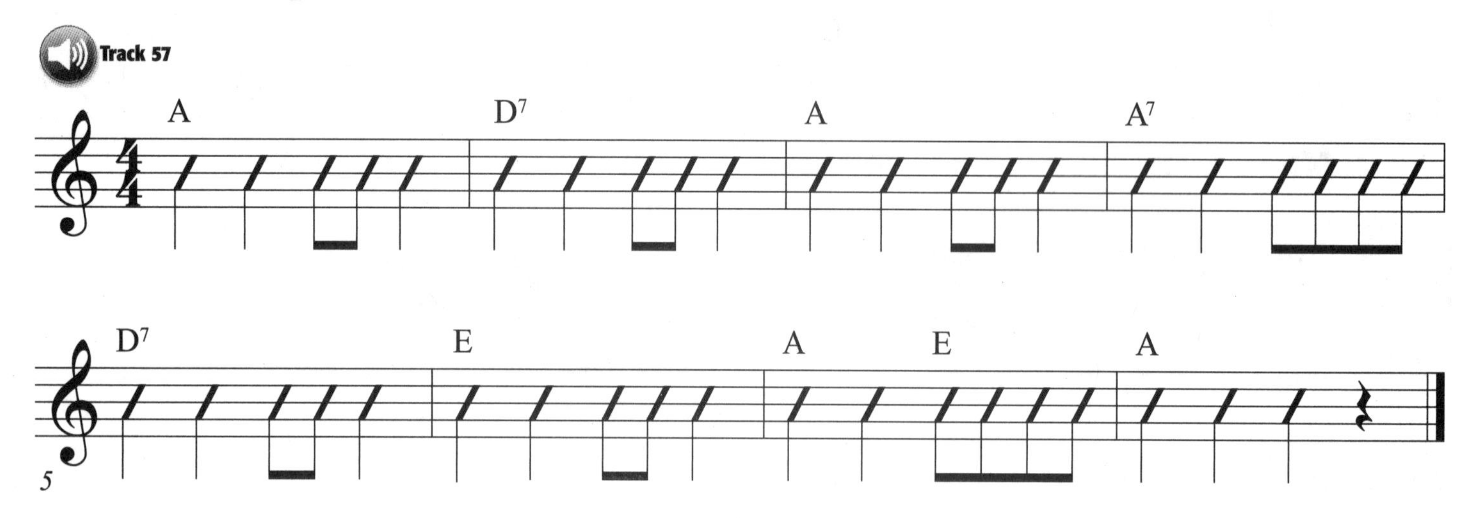

Minor and Major

Track 58

This example uses both the E (E Major) and Em (E Minor) chords. Listen to how the mood changes between the major and minor chords.

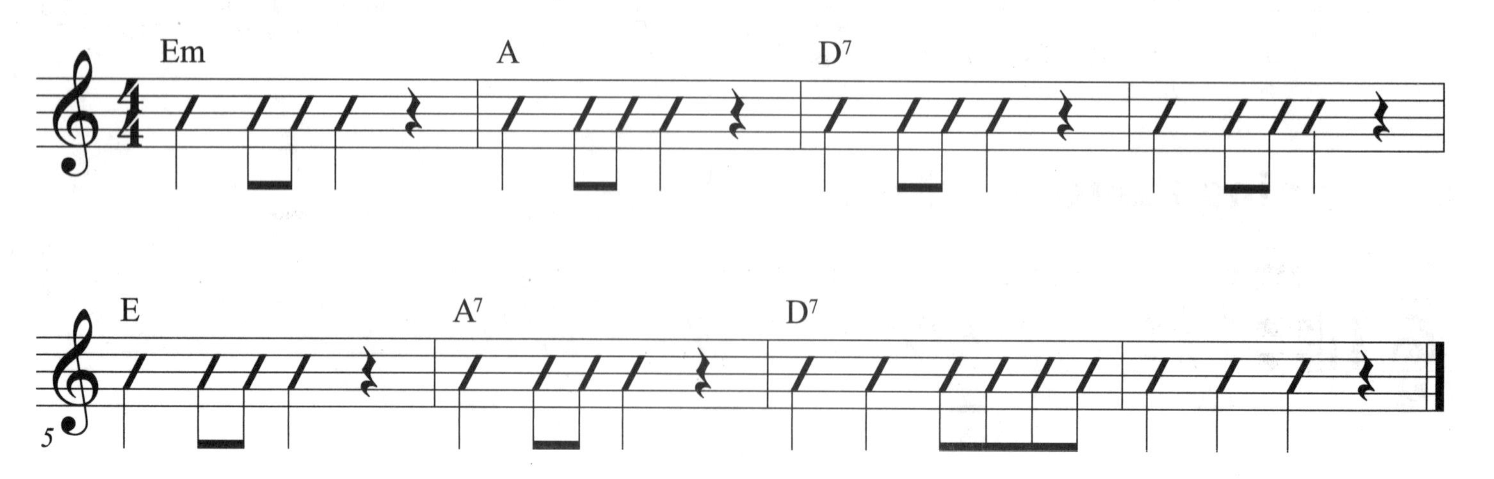

Get Off of My Cloud  Track 59

This was a big hit for The Rolling Stones in 1965.

Words and Music by
Mick Jagger and Keith Richards

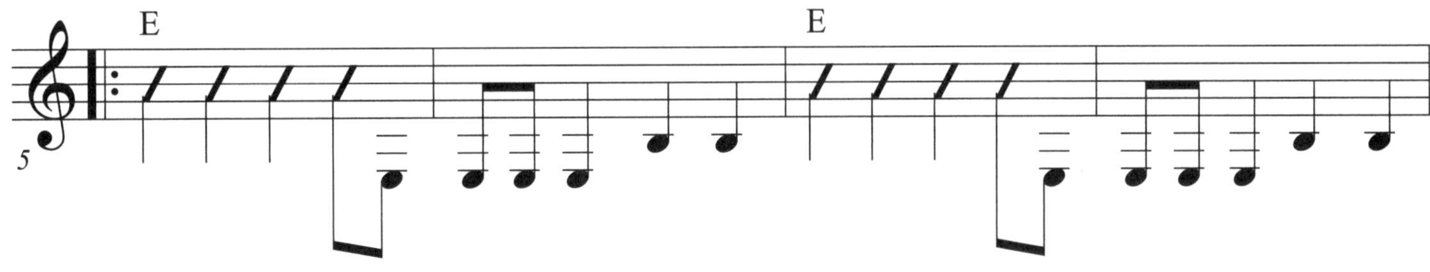

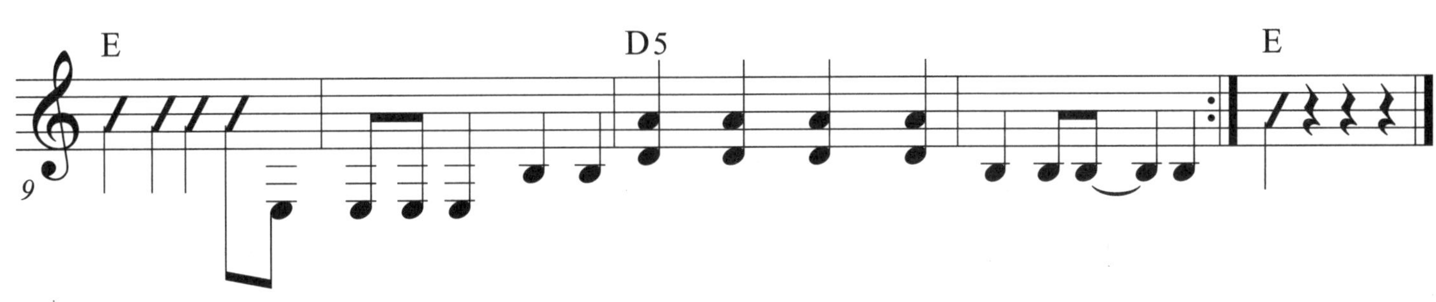

Paranoid Track 60

This song was released as a single in 1970, roughly six months after the release of Black Sabbath's album of the same name.

Words and Music By
Anthony Iommi, John
Osbourne, William Ward
and Terence Butler

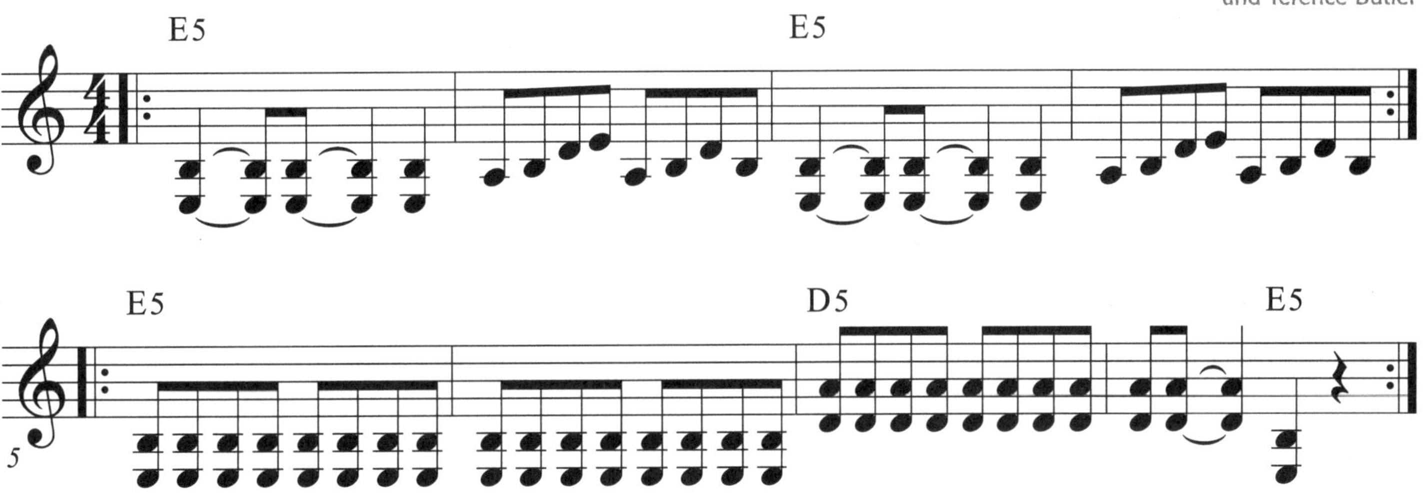

11 Classic Rock Strumming Patterns

These strumming patterns will work with any chord or chord progression. Try an E chord the first time through and an A the second time.

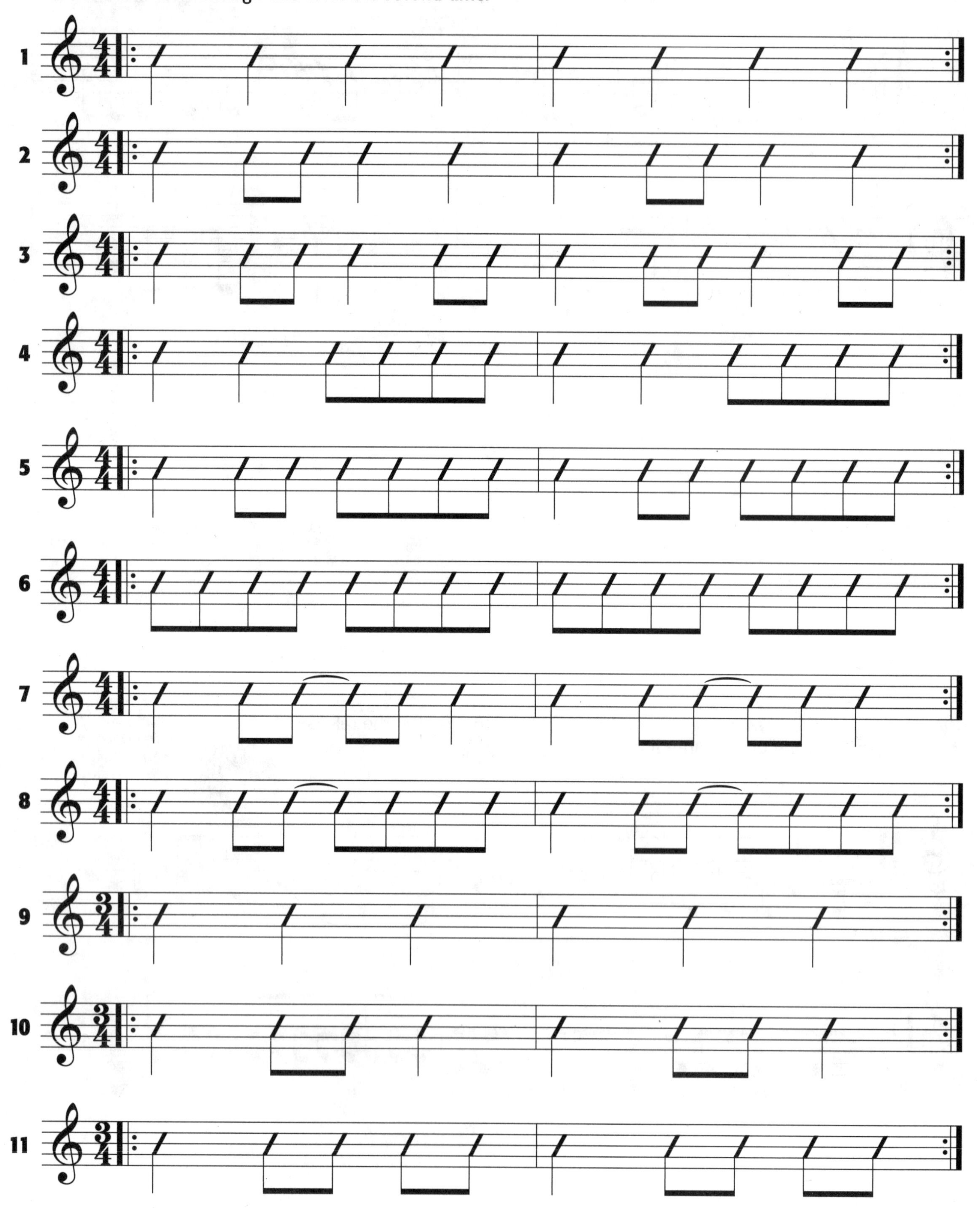

Bring Me to Life Track 62

This gothic metal song from 2003 was a single from Evanescence's debut studio album, *Fallen*.

Words and Music by Ben Moody,
Amy Lee and David Hodges

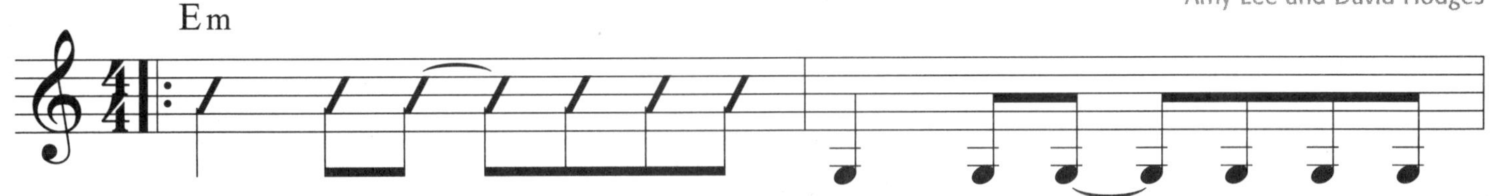

I Can See for Miles Track 63

A single from the album *The Who Sell Out*, this song was hit in 1967.

Words and Music by
Peter Townshend

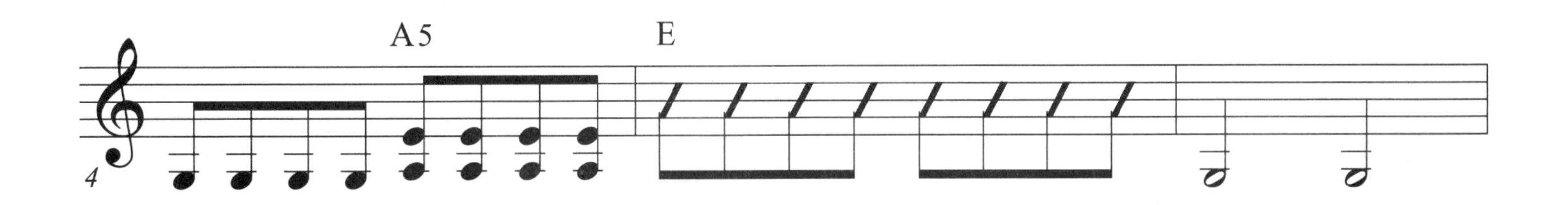

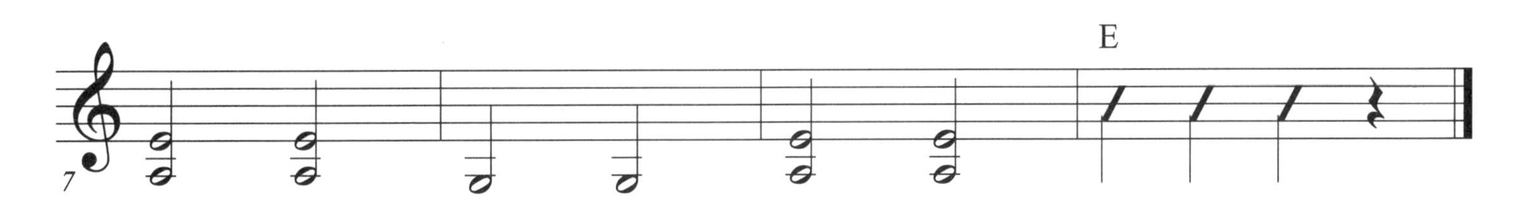

Sharps ♯, Flats ♭, and Naturals ♮

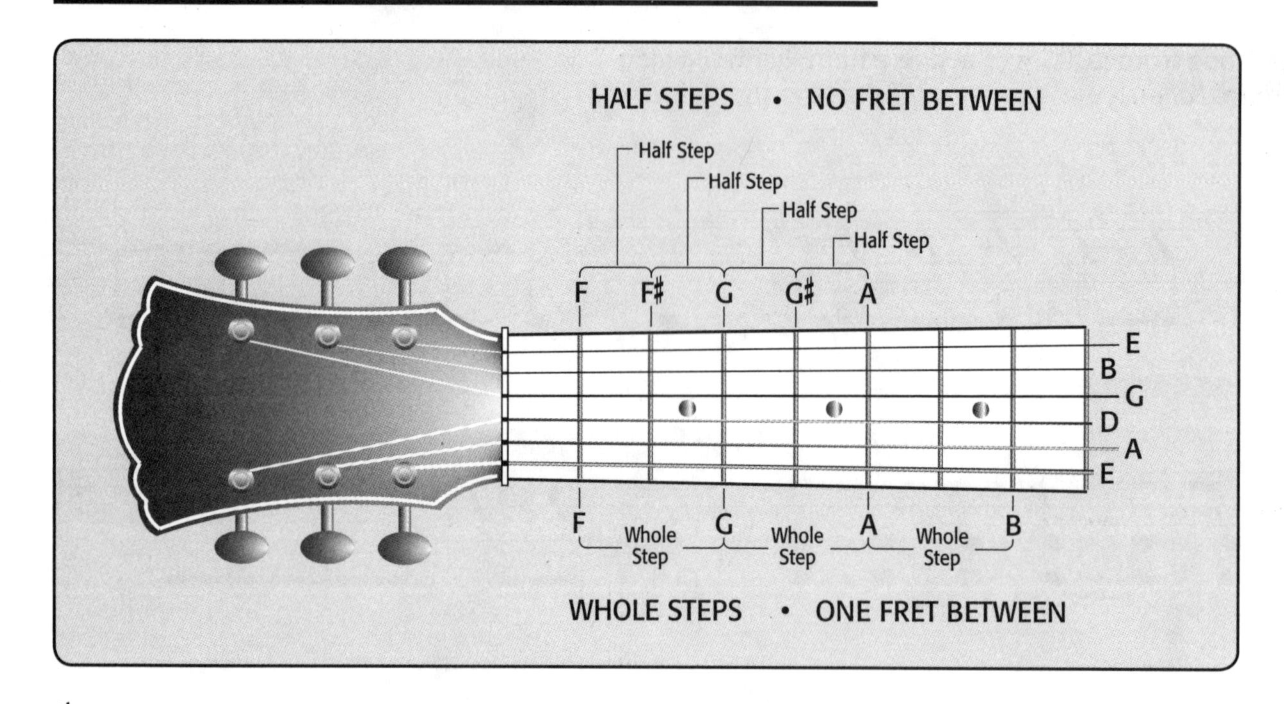

♯ *Sharps* **raise** the note a half step. Play the next fret higher.

♭ *Flats* **lower** the note a half step. If the note is fingered, play the next fret lower.

If the note is open, play the 4th fret of the next lower string—except if that string is G (3rd string), then play the 3rd fret.

♮ *Naturals* cancel a previous sharp or flat.

When added within a measure, sharps, flats, and naturals are called *accidentals.* A bar line cancels a previous accidental in the measures that follow.

The C Major scale (page 29) is created from half steps (one fret) and whole steps (two frets). Sharp ♯, flat ♭, and natural ♮ signs change the notes you already know.

The Chromatic Scale Track 64

The *chromatic scale* is formed exclusively of half steps. The ascending chromatic scale uses sharps ♯. The descending chromatic scale uses flats ♭. Notes that have the same fingering but different names, like B♭ and A♯, are called *enharmonic equivalents*.

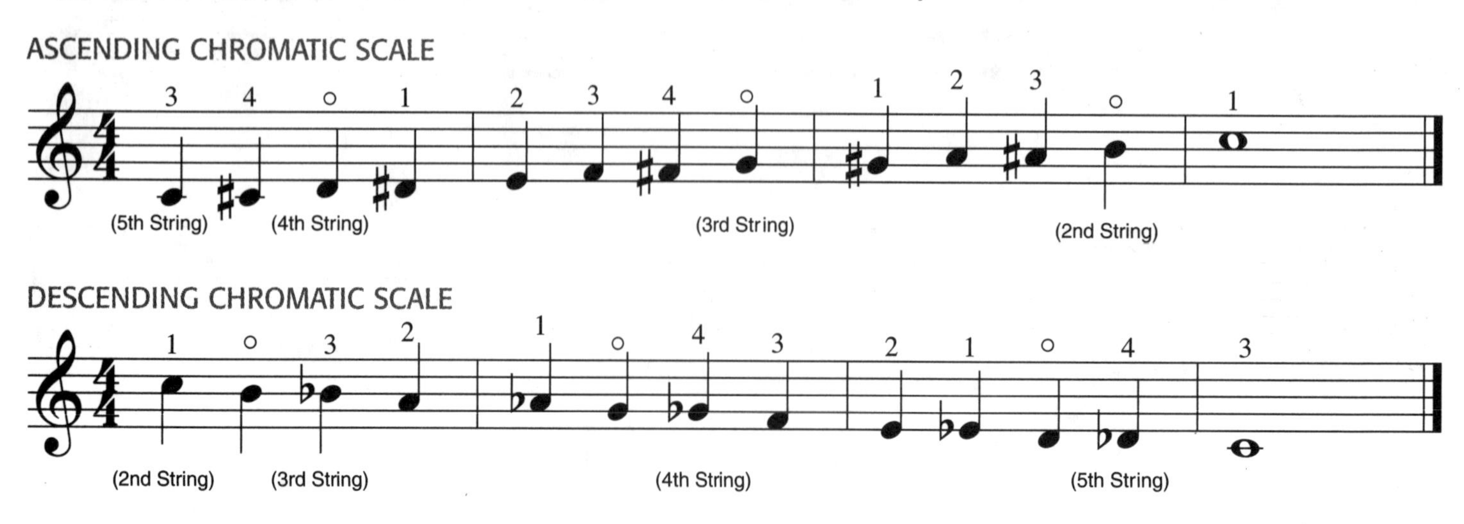

Chromatic Rock Track 65

Before you play "Chromatic Rock," go back to page 29 and play the C Major scale, then play the chromatic scale on page 42 and listen to the difference.

Bluesy Accidentals

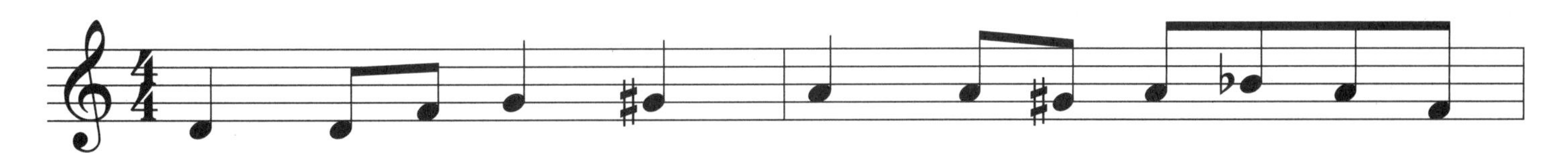

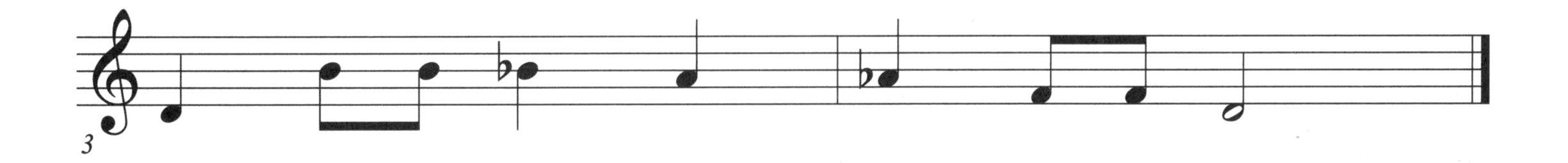

Paint It, Black (Duet)

Released by The Rolling Stones in 1966, this was the first number one hit to include a sitar.

Words and Music by
Mick Jagger and Keith Richards

Signs of Silence

Stop the sound of the strings by touching them lightly with the heel of your hand.

𝄾	EIGHTH REST	= ½ COUNT
𝄽	QUARTER REST	= 1 COUNT
𝄼	HALF REST	= 2 COUNTS
𝄻	WHOLE REST	= 4 COUNTS IN $\frac{4}{4}$ TIME
		3 COUNTS IN $\frac{3}{4}$ TIME

Take a Rest

Track 68

Good Times, Bad Times  Track 69

This is a portion of the intro to "Good Times, Bad Times" by Led Zeppelin. You will be learning a longer version of this on page 62.

Words and Music by
Jimmy Page, John Paul
Jones and John Bonham

Stop-Time Bass Line  Track 70

Playing Two Notes Together: Blues Patterns

E Blues Boogie  Track 71

Most of the rock music we hear is based on the blues. Much of the time, when you listen to some of the world's greatest rock guitarists—such as Eric Clapton, Jimi Hendrix, Jimmy Page, and John Mayer—you are really hearing the blues played loudly with a rock beat.

Start by playing E5 using your 1st finger on the 2nd fret of the 5th string.

Keeping your 1st finger down, add your 3rd finger to the 4th fret of the 5th string to create E6.

Now, go back and forth between these two shapes, and you'll be a blues-rock guitarist, too!

E5 FRET 1 FRET 3

E6 FRET 1 FRET 3

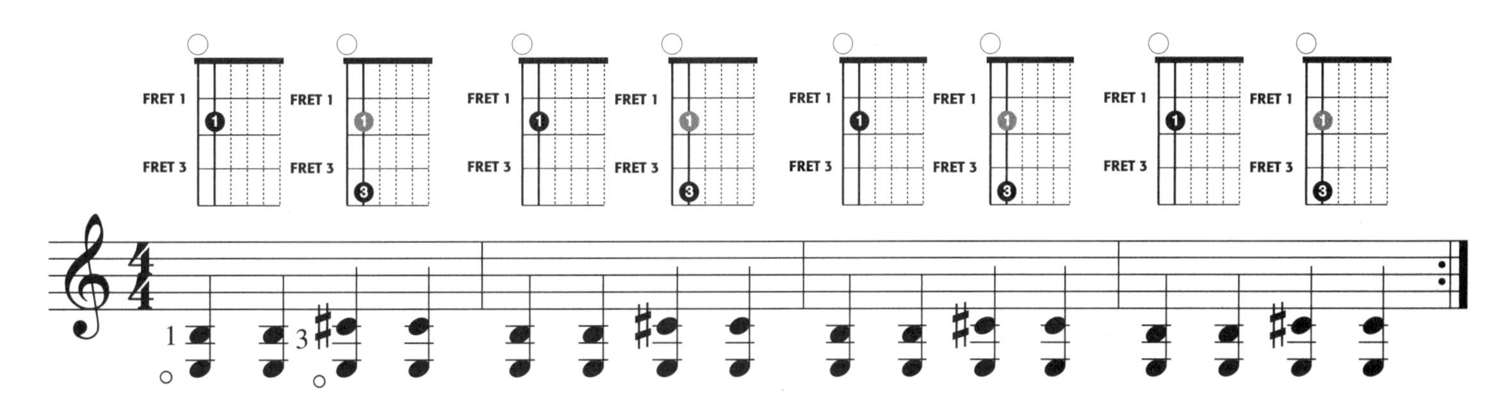

HOLD DOWN YOUR 1ST FINGER ON THE 5TH STRING

A Blues Boogie  Track 72

The blues pattern on the 5th and 4th strings is just like the blues pattern built on the 6th and 5th strings (above). As with "E Blues Boogie," hold down your 1st finger on the 4th string throughout.

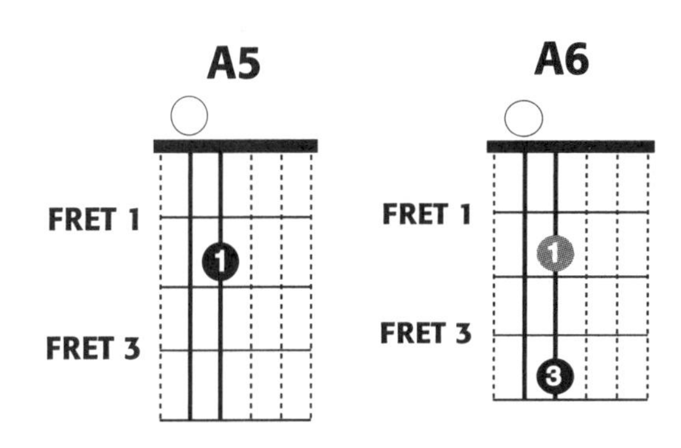

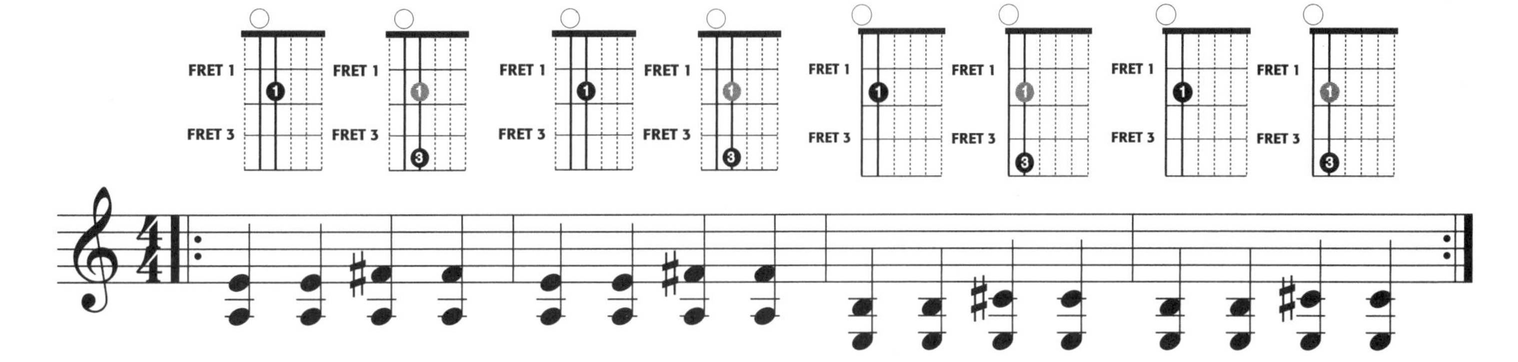

Move Up the Neck on the 6th String

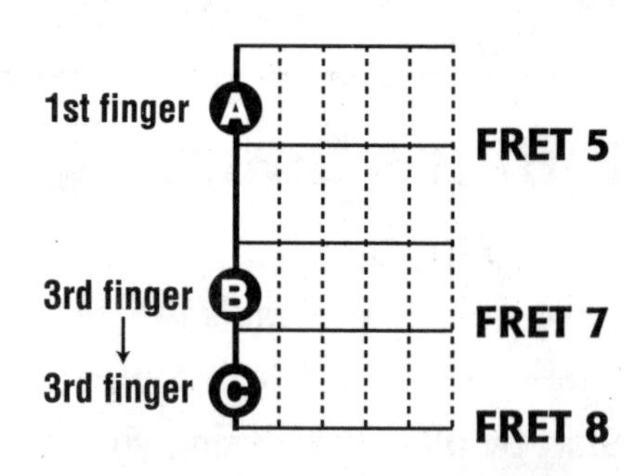

The note on the 3rd fret of the 6th string is G. As you learned on page 8, the next note in the musical alphabet after G is A.

So let's learn three more notes on the 6th string: A, B, and C on the 5th, 7th, and 8th frets. All you have to do is move your left hand up the neck. You can play those three notes with either your 1st or 3rd finger, or even better, with both fingers, as shown in the diagram and photos.

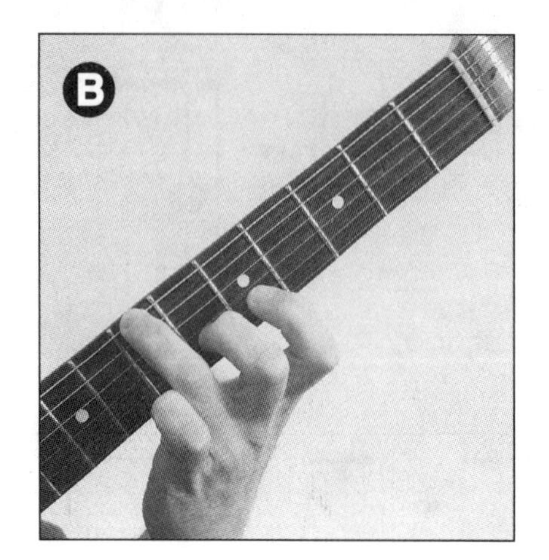

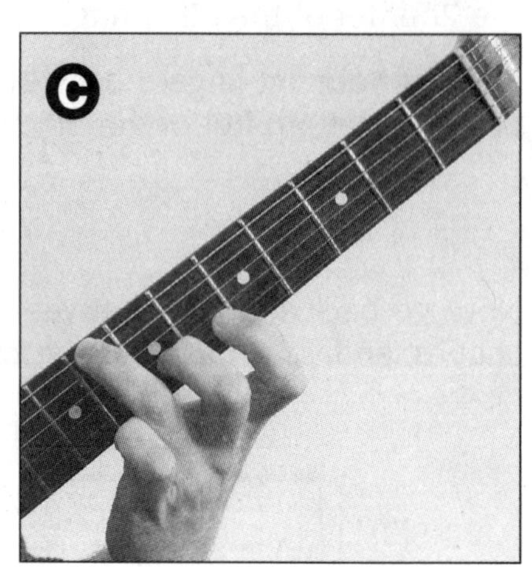

Practice A, B, and C Track 73

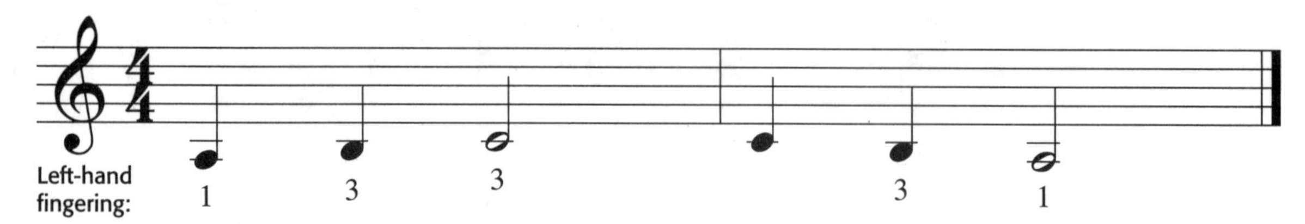

When your fingers move up the neck, you are changing *position*. Position refers to a four-fret area starting from where your 1st finger is located. For example, if your 1st finger is at the 1st fret, you are in 1st position. If your 1st finger is at the 5th fret, you are in 5th position.

In the example below, notice the fingering change on the second count of measure 2—this allows you to smoothly change to 5th position. The lines connecting the left-hand finger numbers show when you are shifting positions.

Two Positions on the 6th String Track 74

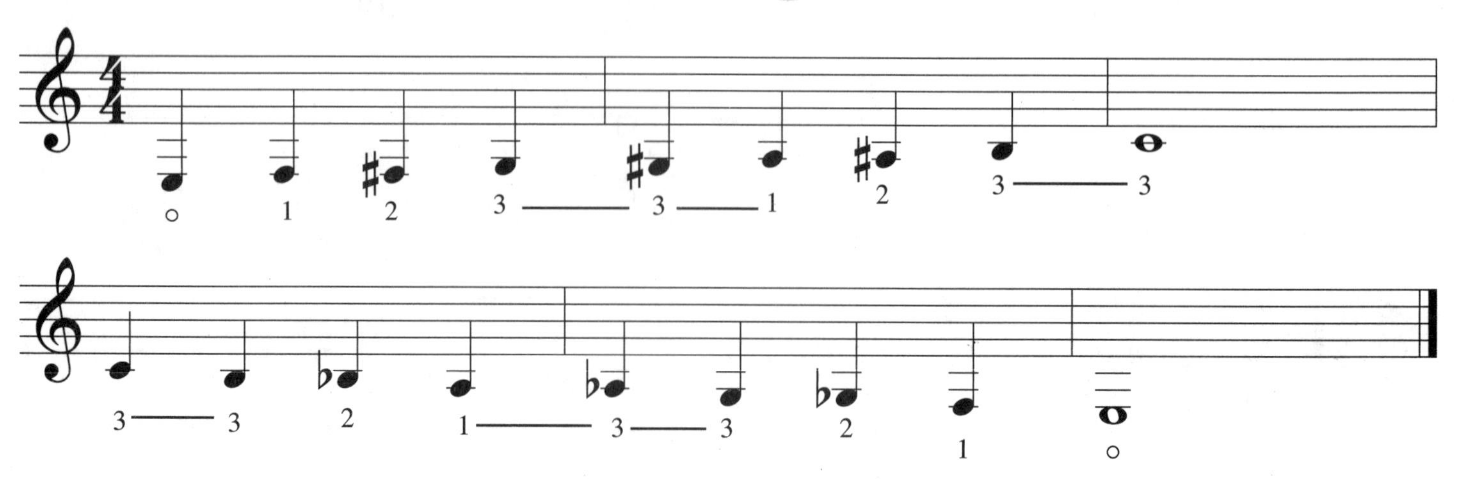

Move Up the Neck on the 5th String

Just as you did on the 6th string, you can move up the neck on the 5th string. And like the 6th string, the next notes in the alphabet—D, E, and F—fall on the 5th, 7th, and 8th frets.

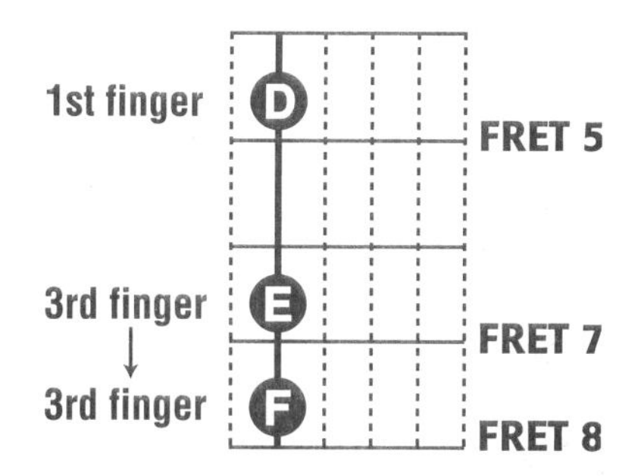

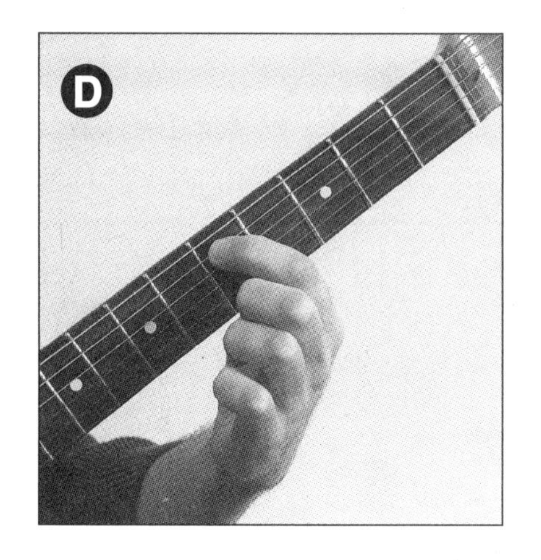

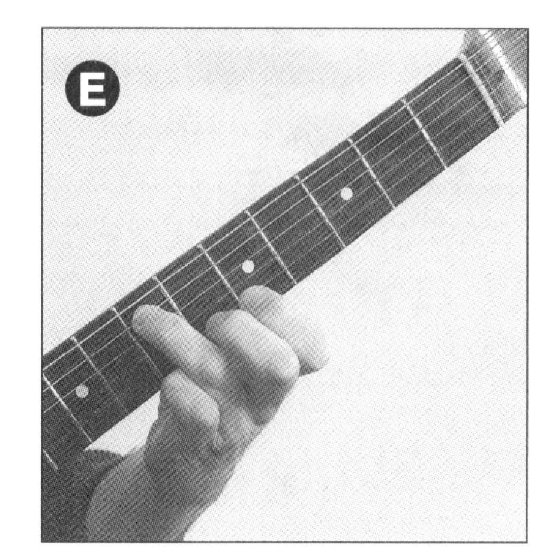

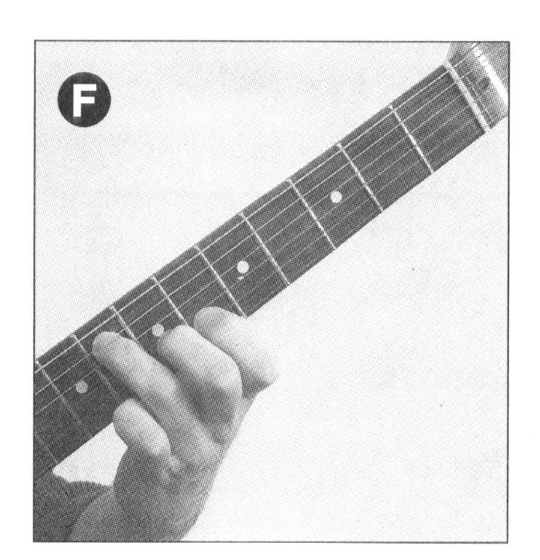

Practice D, E, and F Track 75

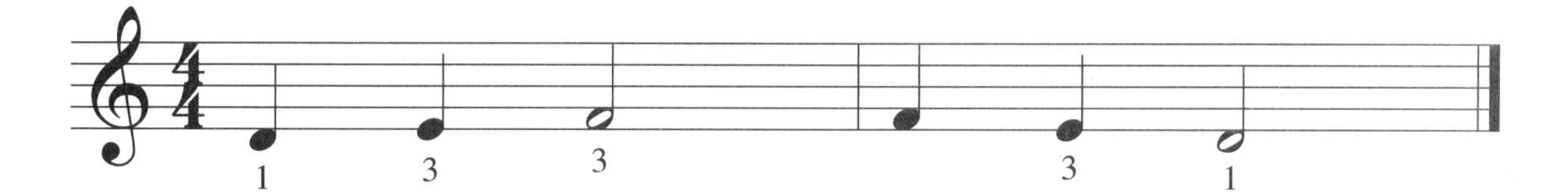

Two Positions on the 5th String Track 76

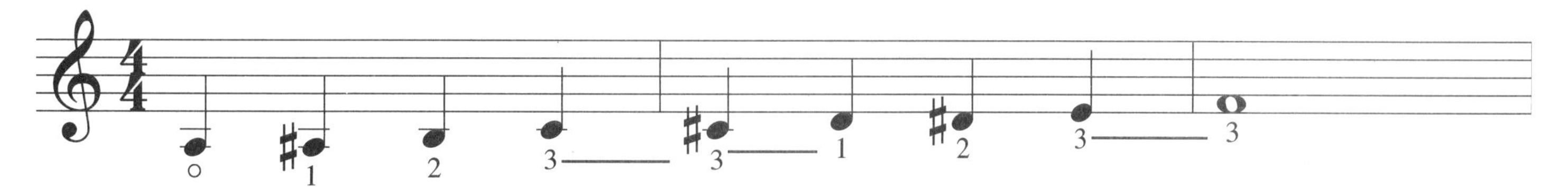

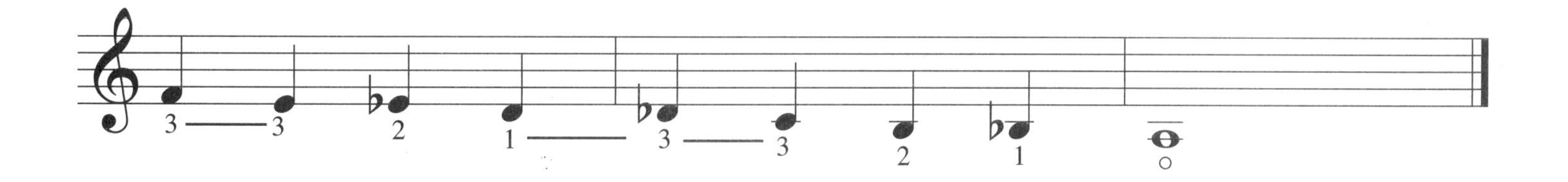

Move Up the Neck on the 4th String

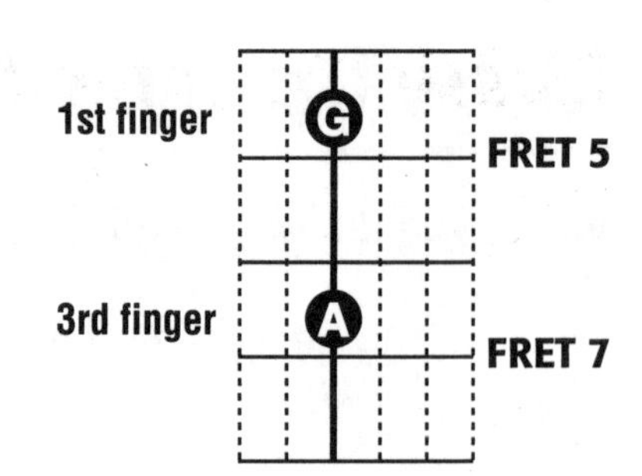

Just as you did on the 5th and 6th strings, you can move up the neck on the 4th string. The next notes in the alphabet—G and A—fall on the 5th and 7th frets.

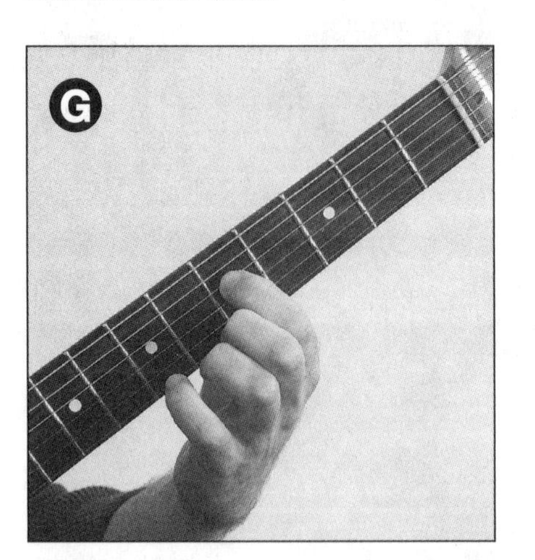

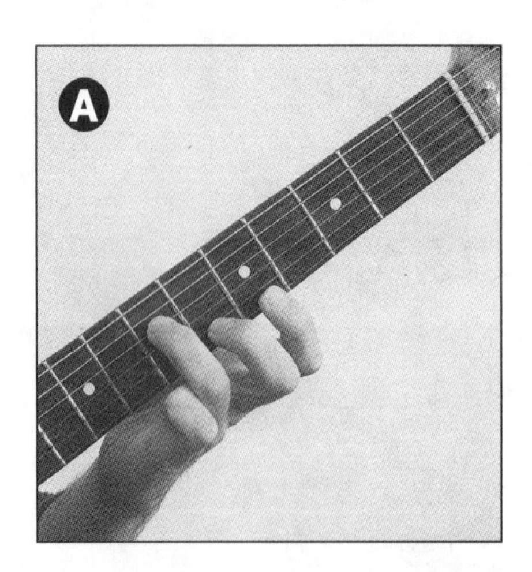

Two Positions on the 4th String Track 77

Move Up the Neck on the 3rd String

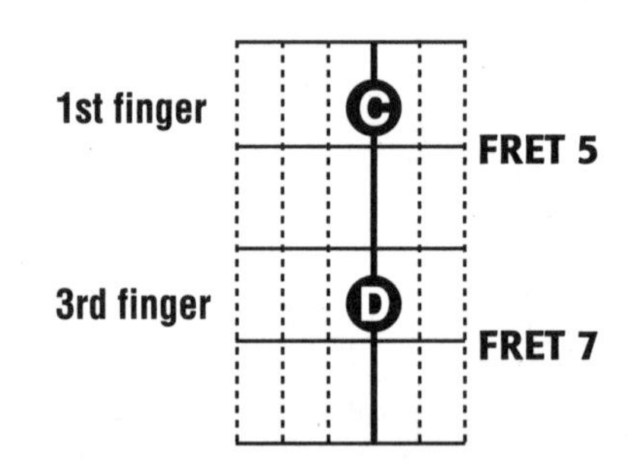

Just as you did on the 4th, 5th, and 6th strings, you can move up the neck on the 3rd string. The next natural notes in the alphabet—C and D—fall on the 5th and 7th frets.

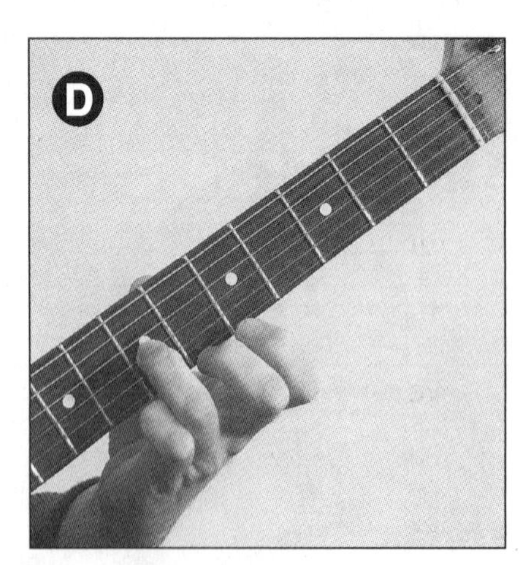

Two Positions on the 3rd String Track 78

Classic Rock Lick with 5s and 7s

Track 79

This is the same lick as "Classic Rock Lick" on page 24. But, this time, play the notes on just the 5th and 7th frets with your 1st and 3rd fingers.

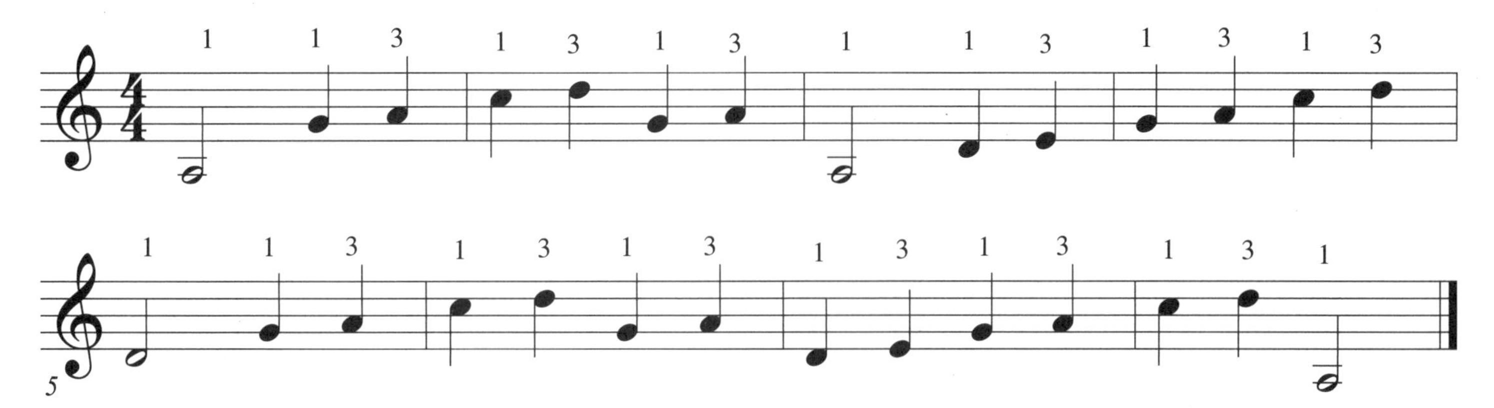

More on Power Chords

E5

E

0 3

B

FRET 1

FRET 3

Since page 21, you have been playing two-note power chords. In a two-note power chord, the top note is five notes higher than the bottom note. In the case below, the bottom note is low E, so the top note is B.

E	**F**	**G**	**A**	**B**
1	2	3	4	5

This is why a power chord is often called a "5" chord. For example, the chord diagram to the right is a power chord built on E, so this is why we call it E5. The E6 chord you learned on page 47 has a top note six notes higher than the bottom note.

Now, try fingering this power chord using your 3rd finger on the B. You'll see why below.

Power Chords Are Moveable

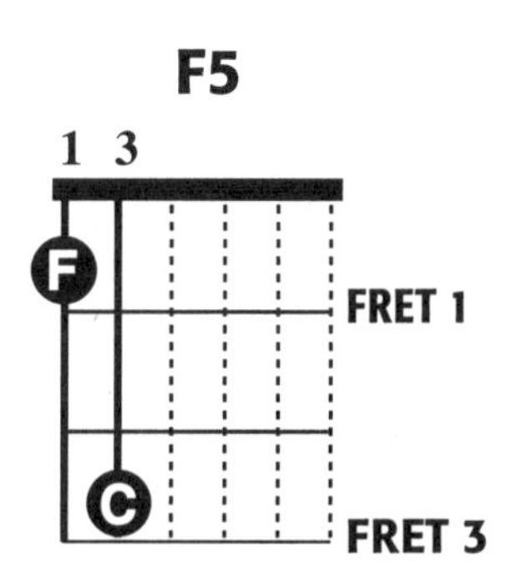

Try this: Slide your 3rd finger up one fret, from the 2nd to the 3rd fret of the 5th string, and add your 1st finger to F on the 1st fret of the 6th string. Play it!

Now, keep your fingers in their positions but shift up the neck so your 1st finger is on G at the 3rd fret of the 6th string, and your 3rd finger is on D at the 5th fret of the 5th string.

See? You can move this chord anywhere on these two strings and it will sound great! As you will see later, you can also move power chords on other strings.

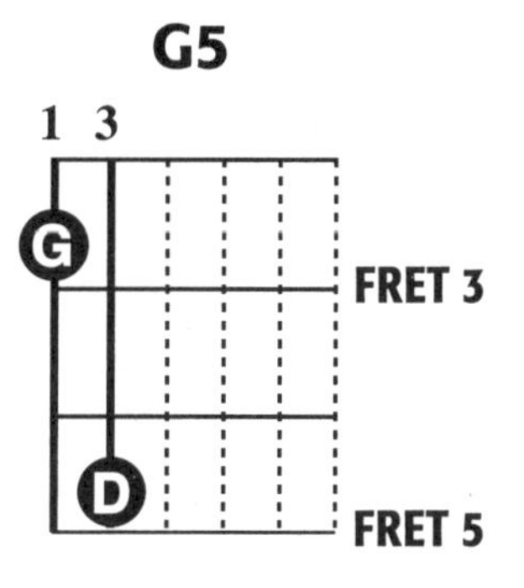

Power Chord Rock

Track 80

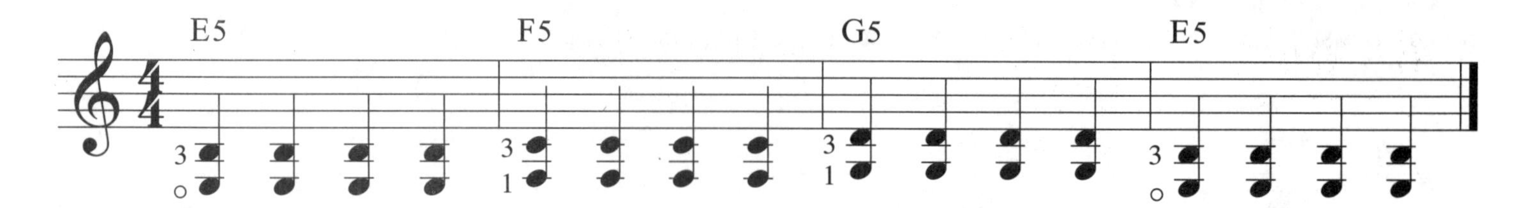

More Power Chord Rock

Track 81

"More Power Chord Rock" uses the most famous blues, rock, and jazz progression, the *12-bar blues*. This 12-measure song form is the basis for thousands of songs, and although it usually consists of only three chords, it can be played in many different ways. This example is a very basic way to play the 12-bar blues.

Count "1 & 2 & 3 & 4 &" throughout, and play on every count. Use your 1st finger on the 2nd fret, and 3rd finger on the 4th. Just be careful to strum the right strings, as some of the chords are on the 6th and 5th strings, and some of them are on the 5th and 4th. Have fun!

Six-String G Chord

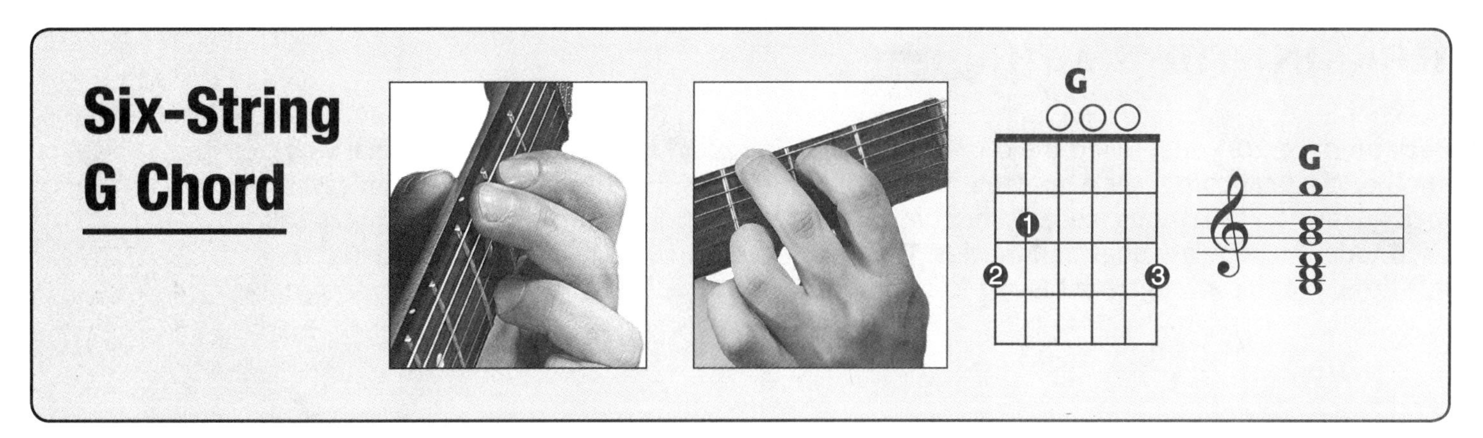

Chords in Standard Notation

If the G chord above feels too difficult, you can use this easier alternative four-string fingering:

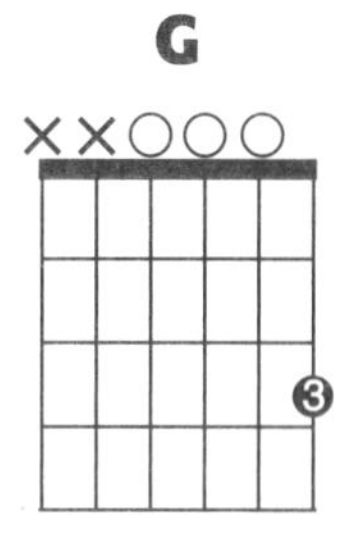

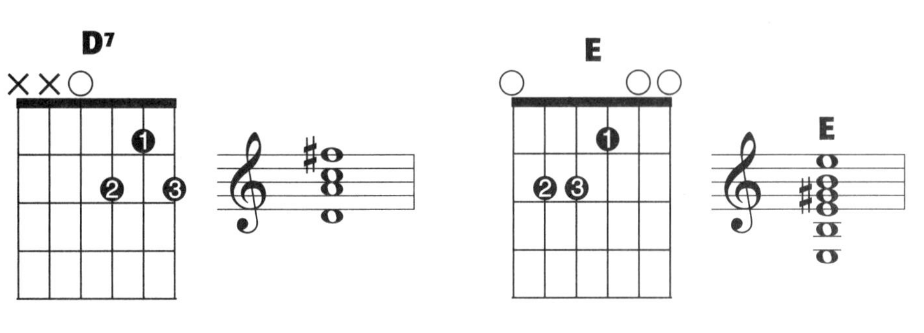

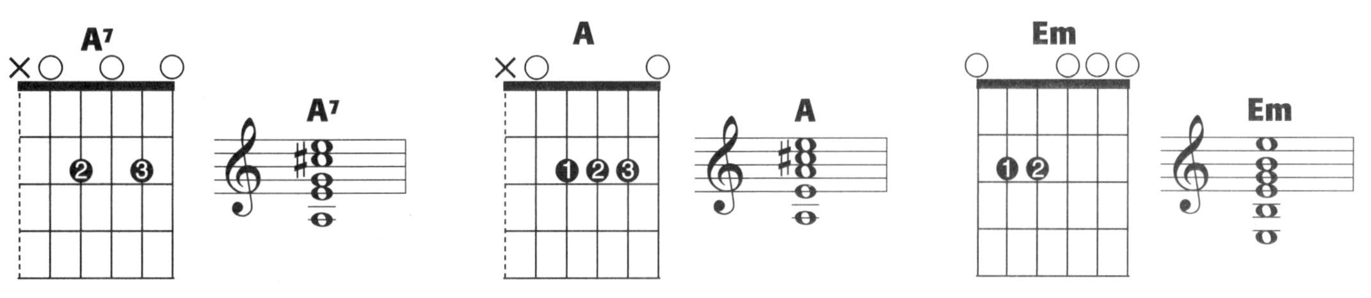

Chords in Notes

Track 82

Rockin' the Bach

Track 83

Back on page 20, you learned the classical piece "Ode to Joy" by Beethoven. J. S. Bach was another classical composer who wrote memorable melodies that have inspired countless rock guitarists. His famous piece "Minuet in G," written in 1725, features a melody that is still used today in popular songs and movies. The original version of "Minuet in G" was written in $\frac{3}{4}$ time, but this arrangement is in $\frac{4}{4}$ to give it more of a rock feel.

Adapted from a Bach Minuet

4

D7

7

10

G

14

Smooth

This 1999 song from the album *Supernatural* was Carlos Santana's first number one hit.

Words and Music by
Itaal Shur and Rob Thomas

Rock and Blues Licks and Tricks

Rock Lick 1 Track 85

Here is a fun lick to play. Learn it and try turning it into your own rock song.

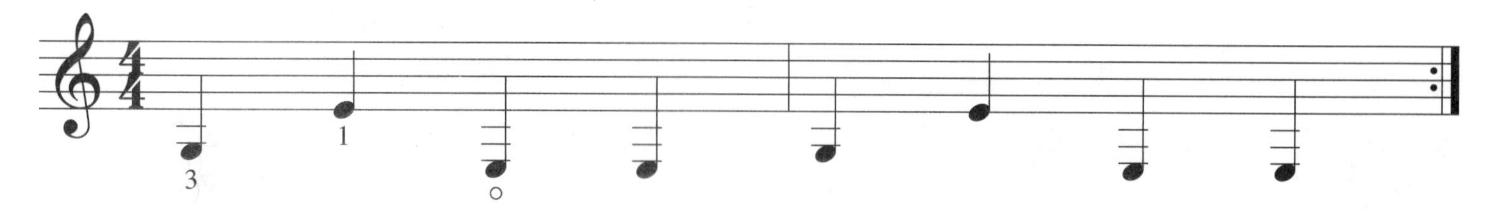

The Bend

The symbol ↗ indicates a *bend,* which tells you to "pull" the fretted string down toward the floor. (NOTE: In some cases, you will "push" the string up toward the ceiling to achieve a bend.)

Keep your finger firmly on the string while bending, and you'll be rewarded with a cool, bluesy sound. Bending is one way guitarists imitate a blues singer's voice, which will often glide from note to note. We can do little bends that add just a little bluesy character to a note, or we can do very big bends. Be careful though, as bending a note too far can break a string. To start sounding like Jimi Hendrix or Eric Clapton, try little blues bends in the licks below.

Low G before bend.

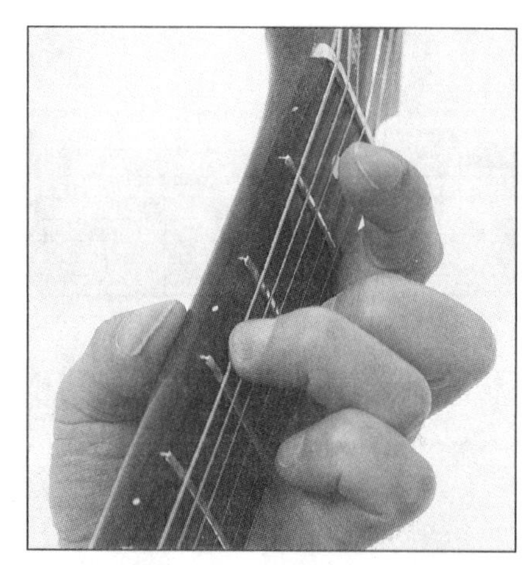

Bending low G.

Rock Lick 1 with a Bend  Track 86

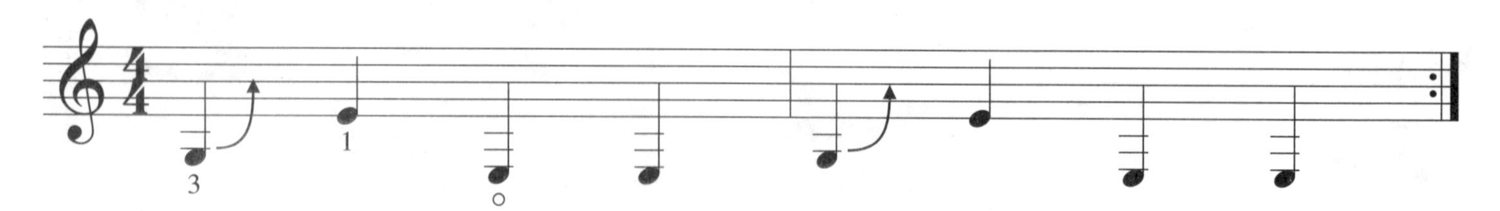

Rock Lick 2 Track 87

The E Minor Pentatonic Scale

The *pentatonic scale* has five notes, hence the name (*penta* is the Greek root for "five"; think "pentagon"). Many rock and blues guitarists consider the E Minor Pentatonic scale to be one of the easiest tools for creating lead guitar solos.

The notes in the E Minor Pentatonic scale are: E, G, A, B, and D. They are shown below on the 6th, 5th, and 4th strings. Play through them from the lowest note to the highest. It's a good idea to repeat the first note an octave higher at the end, as shown below.

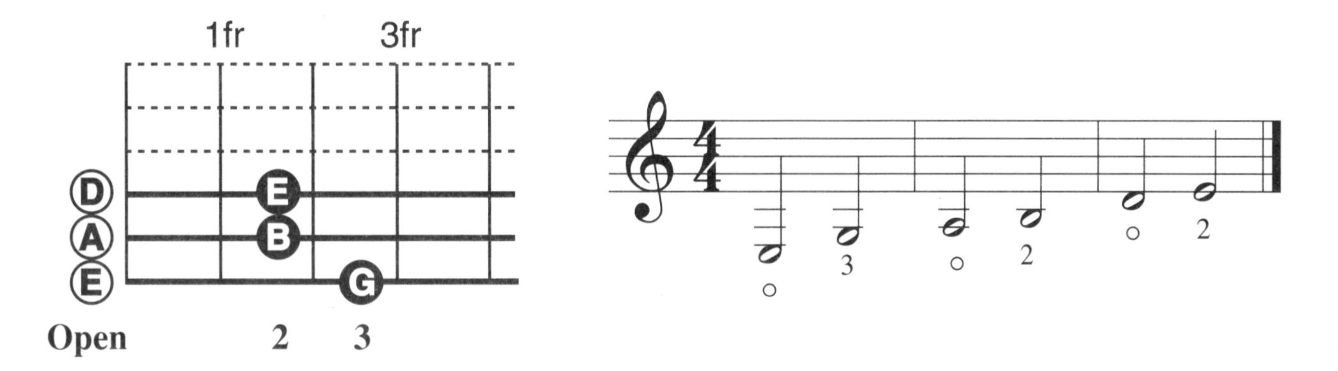

Following are some fun licks to play using the E Minor Pentatonic scale.

Pentatonic Lick 1

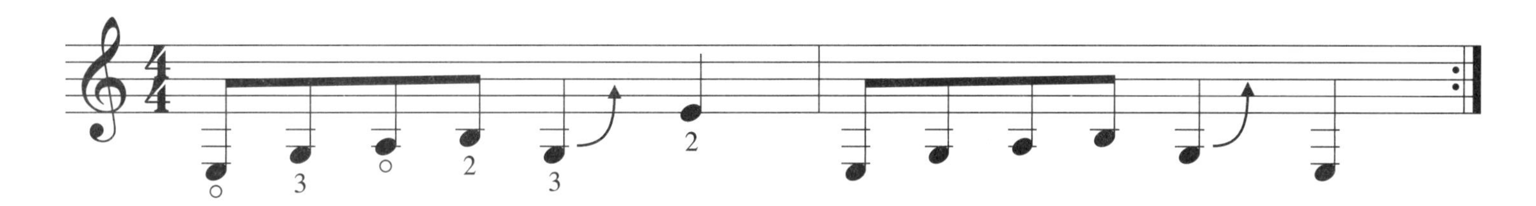

Pentatonic Lick 2

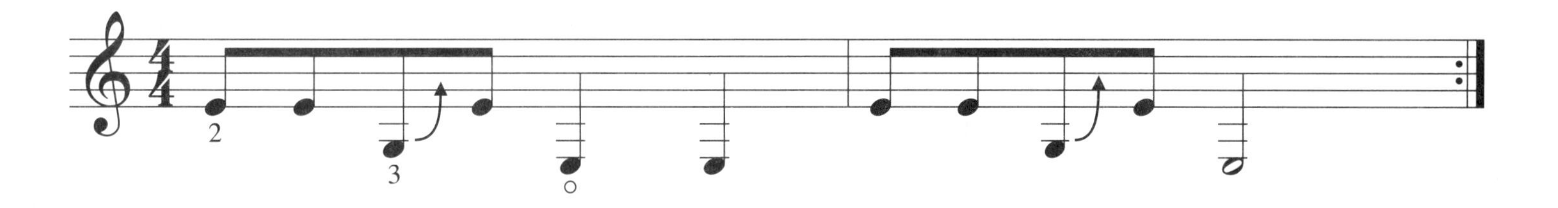

1950s Blues-Rock Tune

Track 90

When you bend the note G on the 1st string, bend up towards the ceiling.

The A Minor Pentatonic Scale

Let's learn the A Minor Pentatonic scale. Since this scale is focused on the note A, the A notes are gray in the diagram below.

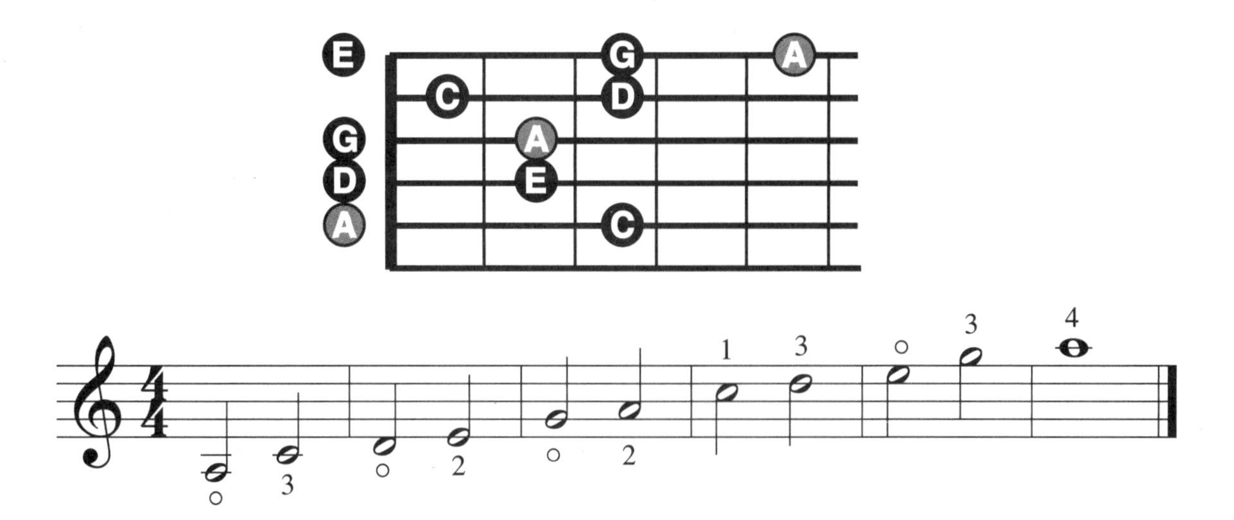

A Minor Pentatonic Call and Response  Track 91

Many classic rock and blues licks use a style referred to as *call and response*, where one musical idea is stated and then is followed by a musical answer that ends the idea. Try this one.

Incomplete Measures, or Pickup

Not every piece of music begins on beat 1. Sometimes, music begins with an incomplete measure called an *upbeat,* or *pickup.* If the pickup has just one beat, the last measure will have only three beats in $\frac{4}{4}$ or two beats in $\frac{3}{4}$.

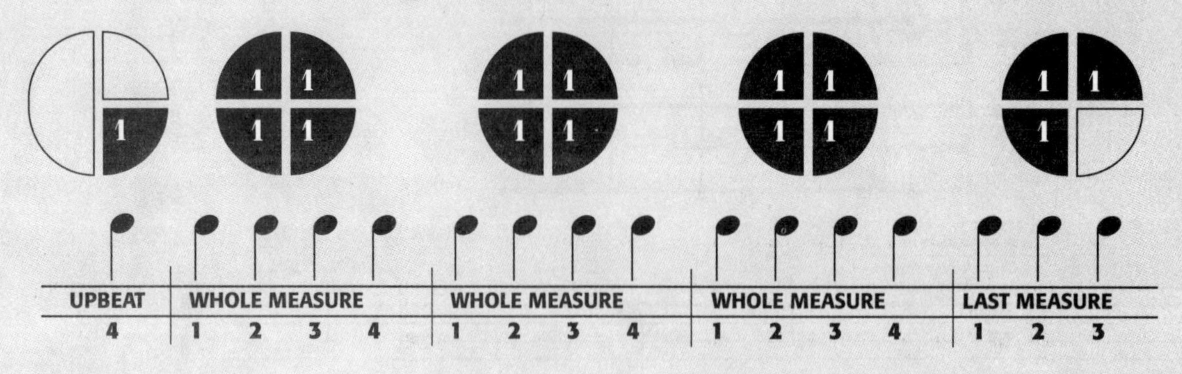

House of the Rising Sun 

Eric Burdon and The Animals turned this traditional song into a rock hit in the 1960s. All the notes are from the A Minor Pentatonic scale.

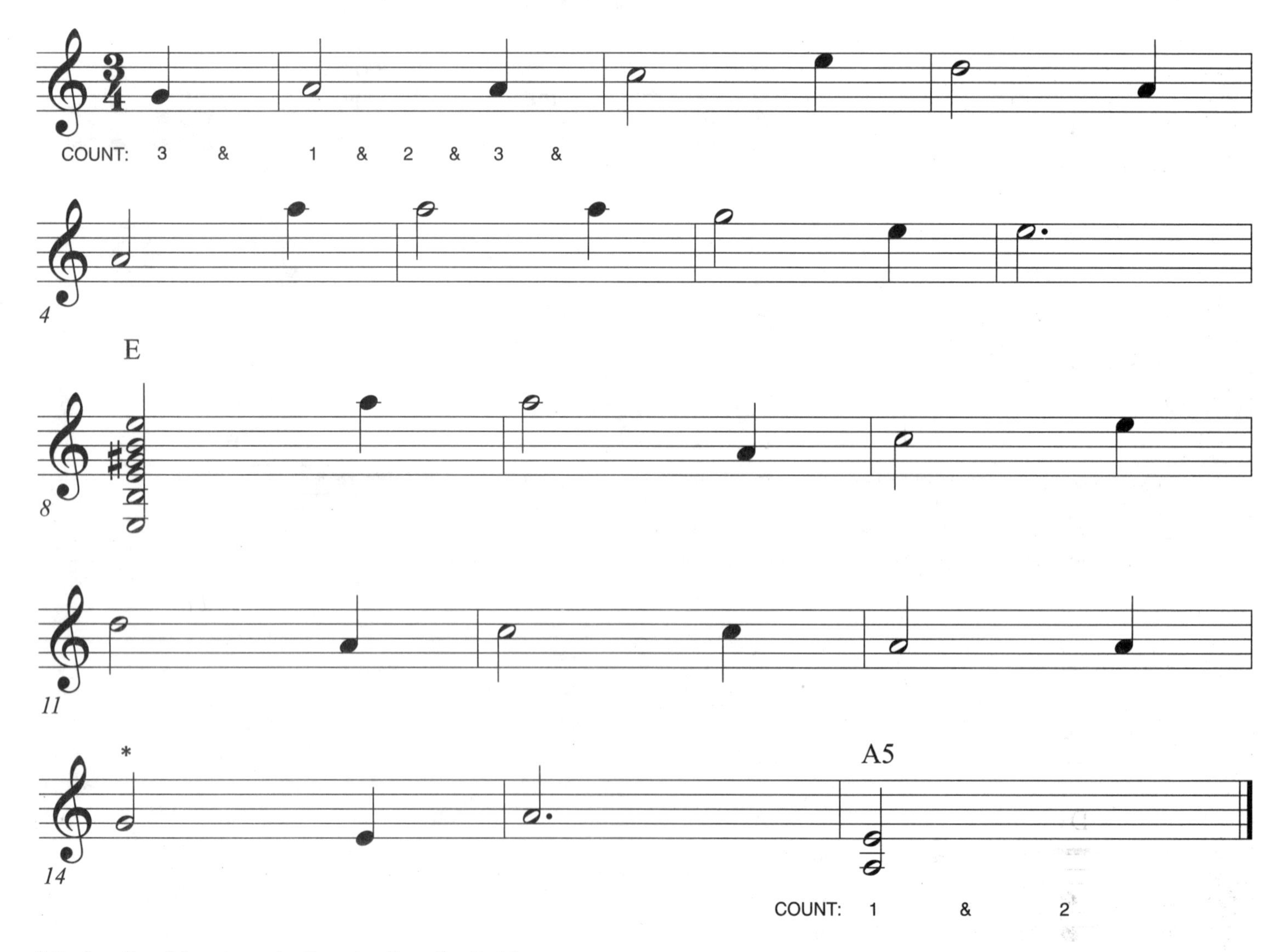

* Try bending this note up by fingering it on the D string.

12-Bar Blues Duet

Track 93

Have a friend or teacher play the lower part while you rock out on this blues solo.

Good Times, Bad Times (Intro)

Words and Music by
Jimmy Page, John Paul
Jones and John Bonham

Guitar Fingerboard Chart

Frets 1–12

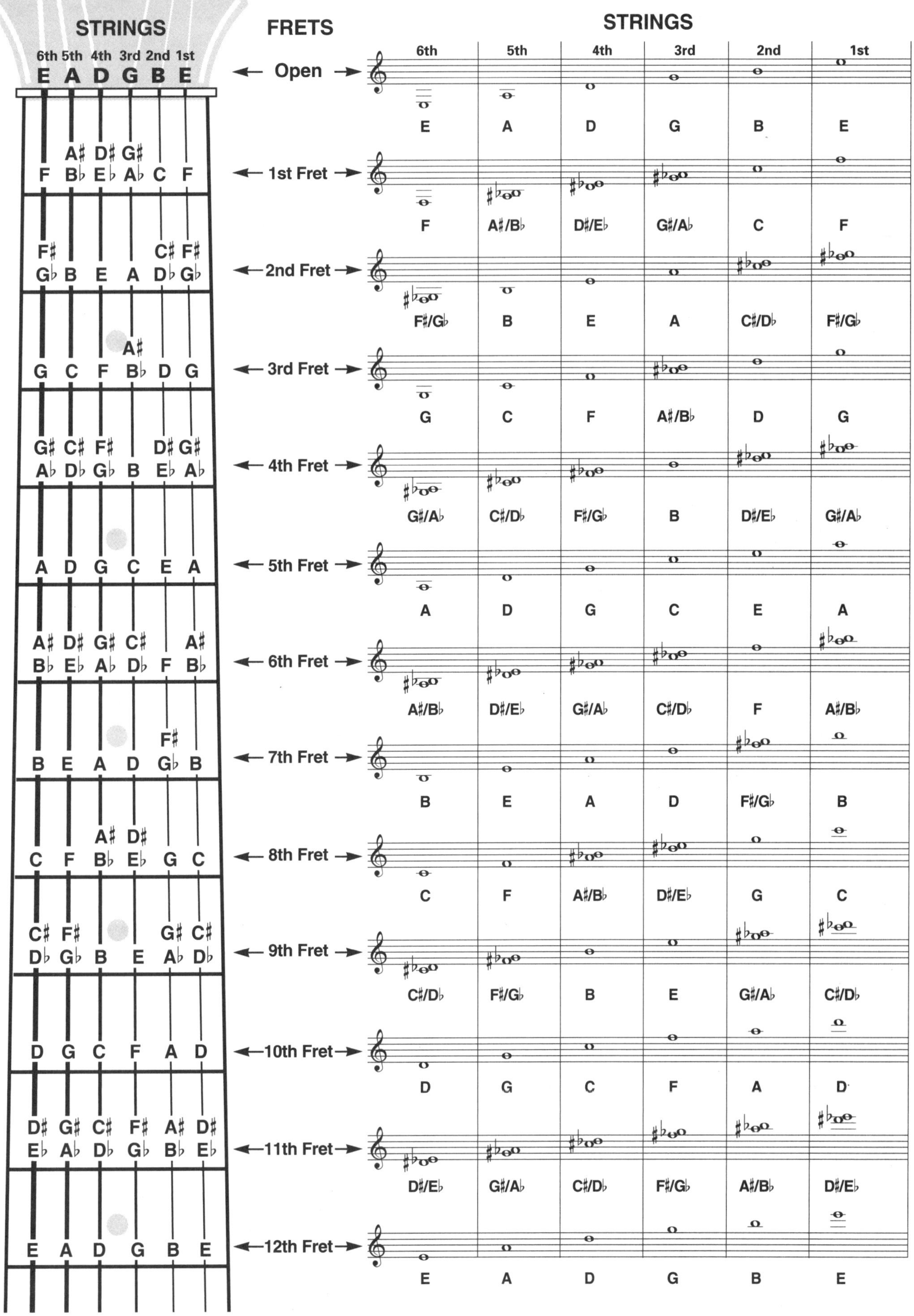

FRETS	6th (E)	5th (A)	4th (D)	3rd (G)	2nd (B)	1st (E)
Open	E	A	D	G	B	E
1st Fret	F	A♯ B♭	D♯ E♭	G♯ A♭	C	F
2nd Fret	F♯ G♭	B	E	A	C♯ D♭	F♯ G♭
3rd Fret	G	C	F	A♯ B♭	D	G
4th Fret	G♯ A♭	C♯ D♭	F♯ G♭	B	D♯ E♭	G♯ A♭
5th Fret	A	D	G	C	E	A
6th Fret	A♯ B♭	D♯ E♭	G♯ A♭	C♯ D♭	F	A♯ B♭
7th Fret	B	E	A	D	F♯ G♭	B
8th Fret	C	F	A♯ B♭	D♯ E♭	G	C
9th Fret	C♯ D♭	F♯ G♭	B	E	G♯ A♭	C♯ D♭
10th Fret	D	G	C	F	A	D
11th Fret	D♯ E♭	G♯ A♭	C♯ D♭	F♯ G♭	A♯ B♭	D♯ E♭
12th Fret	E	A	D	G	B	E

FRETS	6th	5th	4th	3rd	2nd	1st
Open	E	A	D	G	B	E
1st Fret	F	A♯/B♭	D♯/E♭	G♯/A♭	C	F
2nd Fret	F♯/G♭	B	E	A	C♯/D♭	F♯/G♭
3rd Fret	G	C	F	A♯/B♭	D	G
4th Fret	G♯/A♭	C♯/D♭	F♯/G♭	B	D♯/E♭	G♯/A♭
5th Fret	A	D	G	C	E	A
6th Fret	A♯/B♭	D♯/E♭	G♯/A♭	C♯/D♭	F	A♯/B♭
7th Fret	B	E	A	D	F♯/G♭	B
8th Fret	C	F	A♯/B♭	D♯/E♭	G	C
9th Fret	C♯/D♭	F♯/G♭	B	E	G♯/A♭	C♯/D♭
10th Fret	D	G	C	F	A	D
11th Fret	D♯/E♭	G♯/A♭	C♯/D♭	F♯/G♭	A♯/B♭	D♯/E♭
12th Fret	E	A	D	G	B	E

CERTIFICATE OF PROMOTION

ALFRED'S BASIC GUITAR ROCK SONGS METHOD

This certifies that

____

has mastered

Alfred's Basic Guitar Rock Songs Method 1

Teacher ____________________

Date ____________________